Psychic Reiki and Energy Vampires

The Ultimate Guide to Healing Using Your Hands and Psychic Protection for Empaths and Highly Sensitive People

Your Free Gift
(only available for a limited time)

Thanks for getting this book! If you want to learn more about various spirituality topics, then join Mari Silva's community and get a free guided meditation MP3 for awakening your third eye. This guided meditation mp3 is designed to open and strengthen ones third eye so you can experience a higher state of consciousness. Simply visit the link below the image to get started.

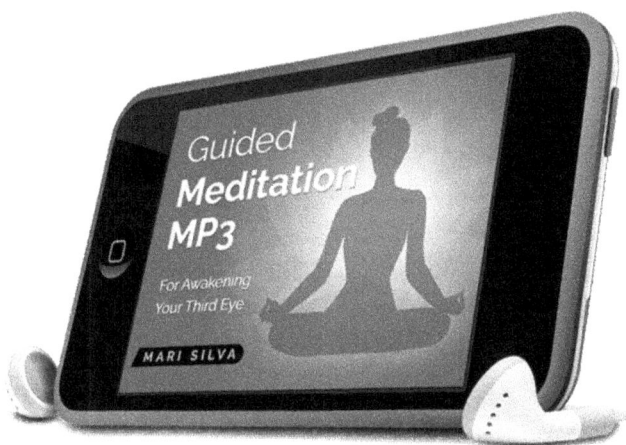

https://spiritualityspot.com/meditation

Table of Contents

Part 1: Psychic Reiki

Unlock the Secrets of Psychic Development and Energy Healing Using Your Hands

Introduction

Many alternative medicine and energy healing therapy forms have gained popularity in the last few years. Yoga, meditation, herbal medicine, and Reiki have proven to be effective methods for helping millions of people in the US and around the world heal and become healthier. Consequently, more people want to learn about this fascinating subject out of curiosity or because they hope to become Reiki practitioners.

If you are a psychic familiar with Reiki and hoping to mix the two together and expand your knowledge, then this book is for you. We understand that these topics can be complicated, especially for beginners, so we have made sure that we straightforwardly present them so that both beginners and advanced learners can understand and relate to the material.

Beginners will find all the information they need to start their psychic Reiki journey. You will find the topic presented in detail using simple terminologies to avoid confusing or overwhelming the reader. We will also discuss related topics like energy, chakras, meditation, and visualization to help you be better equipped and informed as a practitioner.

We want this book to serve as a guide to which you can return whenever you have any questions about energy or Reiki or looking for guidance. For this reason, you'll find various instructions and hands-on methods you can use while healing yourself or others. A practitioner specializing in psychic Reiki needs tools like tarots and crystals to help them access healing energy. However, some new practitioners may be unfamiliar with the necessary items required during a healing session. In this book, you'll find all the information you need about the tools practitioners use during Reiki practice.

You will find all the answers for Reiki, healing, and developing psychic abilities. We have done extensive research to provide accurate information to help you start your career or satisfy your curiosity. Learning a new subject can be challenging. There is always confusion; the more you learn, the more questions you have. However, if your source material provides clear and detailed information, you'll have more answers than questions and build a strong foundation. This is precisely why we have made that we have covered every angle so you would feel a sense of satisfaction and accomplishment after reading this book and be prepared to advance and reach an expert level.

Being a psychic is a gift, a rare ability only a few have. If you are one of these lucky people, take advantage of your unique abilities to heal yourself and others. Let this book be your guide to take the world of psychic Reiki by storm. There is not a more noble cause than helping people. Diseases require doctors, but ailments of the soul will require someone like you with a healing touch. Understanding Reiki and using your psychic abilities can help others feel better and encourage healing.

This book will put you on the first steps on your journey as a psychic Reiki practitioner and a healer. So, let us take this journey together and heal.

Chapter 1: Psychic Reiki Explained

Today, more people are looking for alternative therapies to complement their allopathic treatments for their illnesses. People worldwide are exploring options such as healing crystals, cupping, acupressure, acupuncture, and Reiki.

The last of those, Reiki, is the one that tends to cause the most confusion in people. Many have never heard of this practice, and those who have heard of it often do not understand it properly, leading to them dismissing it as another fraud or fad. However, once you understand the techniques that comprise Reiki (and psychic Reiki), you'll soon understand that it has quite a bit of validity.

This book will take you through the basics of Reiki and will also help you explore psychic Reiki in particular in further detail. When you turn the final page, you'll truly understand why so many people recommend psychic Reiki as a healing technique.

What Is Reiki?

Originating in Japan, Reiki is an energy healing technique based on the belief that vital energy flows through each person's body. The practice helps to relax the body and remove stress.

The simplest way to describe it is that Reiki is performed through a series of gentle touches. Practitioners essentially use their hands to provide your body with energy and do so in a way focused on improving the flow and balance of your body's natural stores of vital energy.

The "patient" generally sits on a massage table during a Reiki session. You will either be fully clothed or covered with sheets or a blanket during this process, and your Reiki practitioner will gently lay their hands on your body or allow them to hover over it. The parts of your body over which the practitioners lay their hands are those where the flow of vital energy is especially potent.

A practitioner will cover your major organs, chakras, and major meridians with their hands, transferring energy as needed. Many patients have found that, during this process, they unwittingly fall into a trance-like state where they experience incredibly vivid and lucid dreams. This experience is so common that it has a name, the "Reiki sleep."

Reiki practitioners often dislike being called healers. They believe that their job is to provide a patient's body with the energy it needs to complete the necessary healing on its own. According to them, people frequently run around low or empty on energy in the modern world. A person's natural energy store is generally expended on their daily activities, such as work and travel.

This means that your body has no extra energy left over to focus on healing, especially healing more than just superficially. That is where Reiki practitioners come in, and they provide your body with the additional energy needed to heal itself.

Reiki is a combination of two words. In the Japanese language, "Red" is translated as "high power," and "ki" is life energy, not just in us but in everything. The name tells new adherents exactly what this practice offers, focusing on the universal, or spiritual, life force energy we all have.

The History of Reiki

Mikao Usui founded the practice of Reiki. Born to a Japanese Buddhist family in 1865, Usui was raised as a samurai and was trained in swordsmanship, martial arts, specifically the Japanese techniques of Aiki, and other similar disciplines. As an adult, he developed an interest in medicine, psychology, and theology and traveled around the world (including the United States) to continue his studies in these topics.

By the early 1920s, he had joined a Buddhist monastery as a priest and monk. As part of his time in the monastery, he spent 21 days on Mount Kurama praying and fasting. It is believed that during these 21 days, Usui was shown the Sanskrit symbols that would help him develop his system of

Reiki.

Usui set up his first Reiki school and clinic in Tokyo in 1922, teaching students the art and encouraging them to spread the practice worldwide. One of his best-known students was Chujiro Hayashi, a former naval surgeon who was instrumental in spreading Reiki outside Japan, especially to the United States, through his student Hawayo Takata.

Hawayo Takata was a Japanese-American woman who initially approached Hayashi for healing in the 1930s. After being healed, she stayed on to learn Reiki under Hayashi, eventually becoming a Reiki master. Believing Reiki had immense value, Takata decided to bring the practice with her back to the United States.

However, as Reiki was a Japanese practice, she was also aware of the challenges that could arise from possible resistance by the public, and the political situation between the US and Japan was sensitive. She had returned to the United States in the 1940s, right before the Second World War, when international tensions were high. This issue would persist following the war's end, especially as the United States and Japan were on opposite sides of the war.

Believing that Reiki's value to the world could not be ignored, she chose to alter the history of Reiki's development and Mikao Usui's life to make it more appealing to the West. She claimed that, rather than a Buddhist with a background in the samurai tradition, Usui was actually a dean of a Christian school in Japan.

Additionally, Usui had developed many of his Reiki principles through studying the Buddhist religious book "Tantra of the Lightning Flash." To make it more in line with the beliefs of Western audiences, she claimed that he had instead been inspired by the story of Jesus Christ, who was able to heal with the touch of a hand and had traveled to the US and other Western countries in an attempt to learn more about Reiki.

Hawayo Takata was successful in her work and managed to help spread Reiki around the United States and, eventually, the world. She trained several Reiki masters herself, who further helped grow the discipline.

Aside from Takata, the only other student trained by Hayashi who practiced and taught Reiki in public was Chiyoko Yamaguchi. Yamaguchi continued to work in Japan, and while Takata had to alter her practice of Reiki to allow for internationalization, Yamaguchi continued to practice Reiki exactly as taught to her by Hayashi. In 1999, she founded the Jikiden

Reiki Institute in Tokyo, where Reiki is taught the same way Hayashi taught her in the 1930s.

Principles of Reiki

Five main Reiki principles may sound similar to other affirmations you may incorporate into your daily life. Let us look at them in further detail:

Just for today, I release angry thoughts.

According to Reiki, the anger you feel at events such as dealing with someone rude to you comes from the anger energy already within you. This Reiki principle calls on you to release that energy by recognizing the anger in your life and letting it go. This, in turn, allows you to replace that anger with happiness.

Just for today, I'm grateful.

This is a reminder to be grateful for all the small moments in your life, moments that you would otherwise watch rush by without thinking twice. If you focus on what is beneficial in your life, you attract positive healing toward you.

Just for today, I release thoughts of worry.

Worry is ever-present in most of our lives. Worry about things that are happening, things that haven't yet happened, and things that may or may not happen. Like anger, Reiki holds that worry comes from within, and this principle invites people to release that worry energy so that they can live easier in the present.

Just for today, I'm gentle with all beings.

This principle is a reminder to be kind and compassionate to all people and beings around you and to consider looking at alternative perspectives to see the world from other beings' eyes. At the same time, it is a reminder to be gentle, kind, and compassionate with yourself because you are encompassed within the phrase "all beings."

Just for today, I expand my consciousness.

Recognize who you are and how you fit into this world as an individual and part of a larger ecosystem. Focus on how you live your life and how that affects everyone around you.

Aside from these five Reiki principles, a few variations are sometimes considered in place of one or more of the above principles. These are:

Just for today, I am humble.

This Reiki principle reminds us that, while our egos would like nothing more than to brag and show off about our accomplishments, we must consider taking things down a notch. Instead, take the chance to bow down, learn from others, and enjoy loving and being loved in return.

Just for today, I am honest/Just for today, I will learn my living honestly.

Though these principles sound relatively similar, they can actually be quite different in practice.

The first, "Just for today, I am honest," reminds you to be your most authentic self as much as possible instead of trying to fit into a pre-destined mold. It is a reminder to let your real self shine and, if necessary, to do so in baby steps, starting with doing so for a single day ("just for today") and then going from there.

The second, "Just for today, I will learn my living honestly," is a reminder to live honestly, without relying on lying, cheating, or otherwise harming others to get ahead. It is a reminder that while money can make life materially easy, it is not and should not be the measure of how successful you are. Instead, you should strive for abundance in all areas of your life, rather than just monetarily.

Just for today, I will honor my parents, teachers, and elders.

This principle is a reminder to celebrate your roots and those who have helped guide you to where you are currently. This does not mean idealizing them or placing them on a pedestal, but rather acknowledging their very real contributions and learning and growing yourself as a person thanks to the lessons they have taught and will teach you.

Reiki Symbols and Attunements

Reiki symbols allow you to use the energy of your Reiki practice for a specific purpose rather than leaving it directionless. They help change how Reiki functions generate energy. They can be activated by visualizing them, speaking their names verbally, or drawing them. The most important part of the activation process is the intention rather than how the symbols are thought of.

You will learn more about the Reiki symbols and how to use them in later chapters, so keep reading to learn more!

Reiki attunement is a process the Reiki master goes through during a class with a student. This helps open up the student's energy system, helping them connect to the universal Reiki energy and become a vessel for that energy to use to heal themselves and others.

The energy pathways are opened through a series of symbols, allowing energy to flow freely through the student's body. Some students report that this process enhances other channeling and healing pathways in the body, with reports of increased intuitive awareness and psychic sensitivity.

Psychic Reiki

So, you are already well-versed in Reiki, but the title of this book is "psychic Reiki" rather than simply Reiki.

So, what is psychic Reiki? Why does "psychic" have anything to do with Reiki?

In the simplest of terms, psychic Reiki is an energy healing modality in which the practitioner's psychic abilities are utilized for healing purposes. You do not need special symbols or movements. Instead, you'll use intuition to direct your energy from your body to someone else's.

In other words, think of psychic Reiki as telepathic Reiki or even intuitive Reiki. It has the same benefits of "regular" Reiki practice but is done without the focus on the practitioner's/Reiki master's physical body it involves. Thus, one can do away with the traditional symbols and hand positions and instead fully trust the Reiki master's innate abilities.

Psychic Reiki is particularly powerful for individuals who are hesitant to be touched by others for many reasons, including PTSD and past trauma.

How to Check if You Are Psychic and Will Be Good at Healing

Are you hoping to get into practicing psychic Reiki? If so, here is a checklist that you can refer to determine whether or not you have psychic abilities:

- Lucid dreaming
- Precognitive dreams or visions
- Awareness or knowledge of people, places, and things that have no rational explanation and are not explained by events in your personal history that you may have consciously forgotten

- Having a remembrance or recognition of your or others' past lives.
- Hearing voices that are not your own or those of others in the room with you or in hearing distance of you
- Having a "built-in" ability to tell the truth from a lie and other such gut feelings.
- Feeling emotions out of nowhere that seem relatively nonsensical until an event happens soon after that explains it, such as a family member calling with good news after a moment of delight, or a friend receiving bad news after you felt down in the dumps all of a sudden
- Experiencing déjà vu frequently and often
- Having people with psychic powers in the family
- Hypersensitivity to negativity, noise, and other people's emotions
- Very sharp senses. One enhanced sense is the most common, though multiple are possible.
- Recurring dreams that you are unable to explain

If you can check off one-third or more of the above list, it is a good indication that you have some form of psychic abilities.

You can also check to determine if you have healing powers. Here is a checklist to ponder:

- You feel most at home in nature
- You are very sensitive
- You feel a calling that draws you to look for ways to heal or ease the suffering of other beings
- You have especially vivid dreams
- You are very creative
- You are very intuitive
- You are an empath
- You can often feel tingling in your hands and palms. This is a sign that energy is collecting in these areas, looking for a way out through healing others
- You have already had to heal yourself or have suffered a life-threatening or chronic illness yourself

- You are a natural peacemaker when working with two people feuding with each other
- You are a natural loner, introvert, or get overwhelmed in public easily
- You have a history of healers in your family. These can be spiritual healers with healing powers or more "traditional" healers like doctors and nurses as well
- You are a good listener
- You can feel the energy within yourself. More than that, you can also distinguish between different types of energy within yourself and alter it if needed
- You have undergone several mystical experiences

If you can relate to one-third or more of the above checklist, it is a good sign that you have healing powers and/or intentions.

This book will cover everything you need to know about honing your psychic and healing powers through psychic Reiki. In the next few chapters, we will walk you through the life force energy you'll be working with and the seven primary chakras. We will also walk you through meditation and visualization, including the hand positions as recommended by Mikao Usui's Gassho Kokyo-ho meditation technique.

We will also explore how you can work with your Spirit Guides and what clearing and grounding are. We will cover why clearing and grounding are important before any form of healing.

We will then help you develop your psychic abilities further. These abilities are often known as the "Clairs," and this book will ensure that you can use them effectively in your practice of psychic Reiki. Then, we will move on to three psychic Reiki practicums so you can use the knowledge you have gained practically and effectively.

Finally, we will also help you explore how you can activate your Third Eye Temple, which can, in turn, further enhance your psychic practice. We will also provide you with a psychic Reiki "toolkit," the tools you can use to complement your psychic reiki practice, such as crystals, tarot, talismans, Reiki water, and more.

If psychic Reiki sounds like something you want to explore further, you are in the right place. All that is left for you to do is turn to the next page!

Chapter 2: Energy and Chakras

Can a chef learn how to cook without any knowledge of food? The same principle applies to energy healers. Before becoming a Reiki practitioner, you should first know what energy is. Why is it important? What is life force energy? Answering these questions will prepare you as you begin your journey to become a psychic Reiki practitioner.

What Is Lifeforce Energy?

Lifeforce energy is a concept that exists in various cultures worldwide and goes by many names, such as prana, Qi, Holy Spirit, ki, anima, inner wind, ruh, and pneuma. It goes back to our ancient ancestors who understood the importance of energy and its role in our lives. They regarded energy as a source you can use for healing and developed many practices around this concept. Life force is a cosmic energy that exists everywhere around us. As it enters our brains, this energy acts like a phone charger that charges our cells and brings them back to life. Everything in the universe has life force energy flowing through them, humans, animals, plants, water, crystals, and even the Earth. Vital for our survival, this energy acts like a heartbeat, indicating whether we are alive or not.

However, energy can be drained one way or another. For this reason, we need life force energy to sustain us. Acting as the foundation of our being, this subtle energy is responsible for every action we take; it defines who we are. It is responsible for all of our body's functions like breathing, blood flow, digestion, and even our body's movements. Life force energy provides us with consciousness and awareness to experience life; without it, we cease to exist.

Life force energy has been mentioned in various ancient texts, which means the concept has been around for thousands of years. Energy is not a modern idea. The world we know today came to be due to an energy explosion known as the Big Bang Theory. Ever since energy has flowed through everything and everyone, this provides an interesting perspective to view the world around you. Everything on Earth came from the same energy, which connects us all by the energy that brought us here.

The Chinese referred to life force energy as "Qi." If you are familiar with traditional Chinese medicine, you may like to know that it is based around Qi which mainly focuses on the energy flow inside our bodies.

We are not just physical bodies; we are much more. We are our thoughts, feelings, and spirit, all of which are connected to the life force in one way or another. Our energies can affect our physical health, mental health, and well-being. Doctors rarely pay attention to ailments that are caused by disrupted energy. So, what do we do when our energy needs tending? We seek the help of a Reiki practitioner. Plenty of alternative medicine like acupuncture revolves around Qi energy and has been adapted to western medicine. Practitioners that work with Qi can recognize the energy in their patient's aura and manipulate it to detect diseases.

The Hindus referred to the life force as "Prana." It is a Sanskrit word that means "breath." Prana first appeared in Sanskrit texts like the Vedas 3000 years ago. In various Hindu literature texts, the sun was described as the source of prana, connecting the four elements, earth, air, water, and fire. Prana, just like its Chinese counterpart, Qi, has a huge impact on our health and is responsible for various bodily functions like breathing and digestion. According to ancient texts, we have various channels in our bodies through which prana flows. These channels are called nadis, and we have about 72,000 of them in our bodies. Nadis are quite similar to the modern description of the nervous system and nerves. Although thousands of Nadis are in our bodies, you'll find three main ones that are always referenced: Sushumna, Ida, and Lingala. These three main Nadis travel from the base of the spine up to the head.

Our senses depend on our life force to flow, which is what heals. We use our senses, and the healing comes from inside, aided by our nervous system, which distributes that energy.

The Subtle Bodies

More often than not, when people discuss bodies, they mean the physical body, which is the most popular concept. However, there is always more to us humans than what meets the eyes. Although we can not see them or touch them, each person has seven subtle bodies, and each one vibrates at a different frequency. These subtle bodies are energy layers connected and encompass the aura. They interact with the physical and non-physical worlds using energy.

According to the ancient Hindu text Bhagavad Gita, the subtle body governs over the physical body and consists of the ego, mind, and intellect. The seven subtle bodies can be divided into physical, spiritual, and astral. There are three bodies in the physical, and they are responsible for the physical plane's energy. Three in the spiritual and are responsible for the spiritual realm, while the astral body is what connects these bodies together. The subtle spiritual bodies are known to vibrate at a higher frequency than the physical ones.

Subtle bodies are not a new concept. In fact, they were mentioned in various ancient cultures like Native America, Ancient Egypt, Chinese, and Ancient India (Sanskrit).

Becoming a psychic Reiki practitioner requires working with energy and learning to manipulate it. You should become familiar with the seven subtle bodies to navigate the spiritual world.

The Etheric Body

Of all the seven subtle bodies, the etheric body is considered the closest to the physical body, located just a couple of inches from it. This subtle body transforms the universe's energy to supply the physical body with what it needs to survive and function properly. As a result of this proximity, the etheric body has a huge impact on our bodily functions.

The etheric body is the densest of all the subtle bodies. For this reason, and since it is the closest to the physical body, it has the lowest frequency. Reiki practitioners should pay close attention to the etheric body because it is directly impacted by various alternative healing methods like acupuncture, Qigong, and Reiki.

The Emotional Body

As the name implies, the emotional body is responsible for our feelings and emotions. Located three inches from the physical body, the emotional body can impact our physical and mental health and our souls because our emotions can affect different areas of our lives. The emotional body's aura is the only one that changes colors and shape depending on a person's mood. For instance, if you are angry, depressed, anxious, or in love, the color and shape of your aura change every time. Once you learn how to read people's auras, you'll be able to determine their moods from their aura's color.

The Mental Body

This subtle body is located a little further from the previously mentioned subtle bodies. Located three to eight inches away from the physical body, the mental body is responsible for our memory, thoughts, imagination, intuition, creativity, logic, and how we gather and process information. It directly impacts the mind, and when it is not functioning properly, it can affect our creativity and concentration. Since our minds never stop working and are always racing with thoughts, the mental body is always glowing in the color yellow.

However, on some occasions, when the mind shuts down, such as when we sleep or after meditation, this subtle body becomes discolored—it can switch color based on our emotions and thoughts. For instance, if you think about how much you miss someone and you get sad, the color of the emotional body aura will change. This affects our mood, and the body's aura will change to mirror that.

The Astral Body

The astral body is perfectly positioned to create a connection between the spirit real and our physical body. Through the astral body, a person can explore the spiritual realm and visit other dimensions. As a result of its connection to the spiritual realm, it is considered superior to the other physical, subtle bodies.

Located one foot from the physical body, the astral body shares a special connection with the emotional body that, on occasions, both can glow the same colors.

The Etheric Template Body

This is a map of our physical self. Located about two inches away from the physical body, it is where one can find their healing power. This template was in existence long before we were.

The Celestial Body

A connection to the higher power. We can tap into this to become more aware of who we are and how we relate to everything else, forging more connections with the universe. Since it only exists in the spiritual realm, the celestial body stands out from its counterparts who exist only in the physical world. However, you can still connect to it and reach the divine when your other physical, subtle bodies are quiet. This usually happens through meditation.

The Causal Body

Last but not least is the causal body located five feet from the physical body. Referred to by some as the soul, the causal body is where all of the information about the subtle physical bodies and your awareness of being one with the divine is stored. The causal body vibrates at a higher frequency than any other subtle body with an aura of a golden color. Once you establish a connection with it, you become aware that you are one with the universe.

Have you ever wondered about people who remember their past lives? In reincarnation, your physical body does not return, but the casual body does. It carries with it the information from the subtle body, transferring it. This allows you to tap into your past lives, though you need outside help to achieve this.

The Aura

We have mentioned the aura a few times while discussing the subtle bodies, but what is the aura? Each living being is surrounded by an invisible energy field that changes colors to reflect their spiritual and emotional well-being. This energy field is the aura. Aura is invisible to the naked eye, but many people can sense other peoples' auras, often referred to as a vibe. For instance, you can meet someone and feel they "radiate" a warm and friendly vibe? What you are sensing here is their aura. You can still see your or other people's aura through peripheral vision, but it requires practice. Inside the aura is where the seven subtle bodies exist, each one forming a different layer.

Exercise

Now that you have familiarized yourself with the aura and subtle body, let us test what you have learned. As a Reiki practitioner, learning to harness energy through your hands is a skill you should master. Creating a chi ball is one of the best methods to help you focus and direct energy. You will need another person with you for this practice.

Directions

- Stand up straight
- Relax your body and mind, and inhale deeply
- Clear your thoughts and slowly exhale while focusing on your navel area. This step will help you be centered
- Now, imagine there are chords of energy stuck to your feet, acting as roots in the floor. This step will make you feel grounded and help you remain focused
- Rub your palms together until they feel warm
- Next, place your palms close together, facing each other as if you are about to clap
- Move your palms about a foot apart from each other slowly, then move them close to each other again
- Repeat this previous step a few times until you begin to feel resistance. This resistance is the energy
- Using your cupped hands, mold the energy into a ball by moving your palms back and forth
- Visualize this ball of energy as a healing light
- Make sure that the other person is sitting or lying down in a relaxed position
- Visualize the color of the healing ball. Do not overthink it, simply choose a color you feel drawn to or a mix of rainbow colors
- Set an intention for the healing ball, such as the person's name, positive thoughts, or the area of the body that requires healing
- Now place the energy ball above the other person's head
- Slowly and gently, push the ball down, visualize it entering their body, and visualize their body being filled with light
- End the exercise by silently expressing gratitude for the healing the person you helped has received

Chakras

Chakra map.
mpan, CC0, via Wikimedia Commons https://commons.wikimedia.org/wiki/File:Chakras_map.svg

Chakras are the body's energy centers, and they first appeared in ancient Vedic texts. Chakras are the channels that distribute the life force by connecting with the Nadis. You will find this in the astral body's spine, our energy inhabiting our physical self, but this is not something tangible. The chakras move up the spine to the top of our head. Like the astral body, the chakras are invisible and cannot be touched.

There is a chakra responsible for every body part of the physical body. There are seven main chakras, and each one radiates different energy and color. Chakras can get blocked or imbalanced where the energy gets stagnant and unable to flow through the spine. Blocked chakras can manifest as symptoms affecting your body, mind, and spirit. Various things can cause a blockage to the chakras, like stress, destructive habits, or poor diet. However, changes in your lifestyle and practicing yoga, meditation, and breathing exercises can help unblock the chakras.

Root Chakra

Location: The base of the spine

Sanskrit Name: Muladhara chakra

Color: Red

Sound: Lam

Functions: The root chakra is responsible for certain bodily functions and body parts like the large intestine, bones, adrenal glands, feet, and legs. This chakra aids us in survival, safety, security, stability, and ambition. Being grounded is the main theme of this chakra which is why it is connected with anything that satisfies our basic needs, such as shelter, food, and water. The root chakra is also responsible for our basic emotional needs, such as feeling safe and secure. As human beings, meeting our basic needs can make us feel more relaxed and can greatly impact our well-being.

Symptoms of a Blocked Root Chakra

- Laziness
- Depression
- Feelings isolated and disconnected from the world
- Anxiety or panic attacks
- Nightmares
- Insecurity and feeling unsafe
- Inability to take action
- Insomnia
- Issues with the reproductive system or digestive system
- Pains and aches all over your body for no reason
- Experiencing health issues with various parts of your body like the lower back, legs, bladder, or colon

Sacral Chakra

Location: Lower abdomen. Above the pubic bone and below the navel

Sanskrit Name: Svadhishthana chakra

Color: Orange

Sound: Vam

Functions: The sacral chakra is all about having fun, which governs our sense of pleasure, passions, and all emotions related to joy. It is also connected to sexual desire and creativity. This chakra provides energy to the reproductive organs and glands, the kidneys, the circulatory system, and the bladder. When this chakra is open, you feel like your best self. You are passionate about everything in life, such as your love life and work. You also become friendly, successful, and thus fulfilled with your life. As a result, your well-being improves, and you experience feelings of joy, abundance, and wellness.

Symptoms of a Blocked Sacral Chakra

- Insecurity
- Depression
- Fatigue
- Emotional instability
- Low libido
- Fear of having pleasure or change
- Detachment
- Feeling uninspired and less creative
- Dangerous behavior like addiction
- Anemia
- PMS (premenstrual syndrome)
- Arthritis
- Less energetic
- Issues with the hips, spleen, genitals, or kidneys
- Joint pain
- Chronic pain in the lower back
- Sexual problems
- Fertility issues

Solar Plexus Chakra

Location: Lower abdomen. Between the navel and rib cage

Sanskrit Name: Manipura chakra

Color: Yellow

Sound: Ram

Functions: Confidence, personal power, willpower, and empowerment are some powerful feelings that the solar plexus chakra governs. This chakra is also responsible for the pancreas, digestive system, adrenals, and muscles.

Symptoms of a Blocked Solar Plexus Chakra

- Trust issues
- Constantly worrying about how others perceive you
- Low self-esteem
- Neediness
- Seeking approval from others
- Feeling unhealthy attachment to the people in your life
- Inability to express yourself
- Controlling behavior
- Playing the victim
- Lack of direction
- Struggling to make decisions
- Anger issues
- Procrastination
- Apathy
- Self-doubt
- Digestive issues like constipation
- Stomach aches
- Diabetes
- Eating disorders
- Ulcers
- Issues with colon, liver, and pancreas

Heart Chakra

Location: In the heart region

Sanskrit Name: Anahata chakra

Color: Green

Sound: Yam

Functions: Since this is the heart chakra, it rules over the heart and all feelings related to love, whether loving other people or self-love. As the fourth chakra, the heart chakra is in a unique position, the halfway point of the seven chakras. It bridges the upper and lower chakras to bring together their physical and spiritual aspects. This chakra is responsible for feelings of compassion, forgiveness, awareness, joy, empathy, self-love, peace, trust, generosity, change, transformation, harmony, self-acceptance, happiness, joy, motivation, and love. Simply put, it rules over many positive emotions. When open, love can flow in both directions. The heart chakra supplies energy to the heart, thymus gland, lungs, hands, and arms.

Symptoms of a Blocked Heart Chakra

- Codependency in your relationships
- Fear of rejection
- Feeling distant from the people in your life
- Trust and commitment issues
- Acting tough when feeling vulnerable
- Inability to give and receive love
- Jealousy
- Anger
- Grief
- Fear of betrayal
- Hatred towards others and yourself
- Feeling stuck and obsessed with the past
- Relationships issues
- Inability to forgive
- Feeling emotionally closed off
- Depression and anxiety
- Victim mentality

- Loneliness
- Shyness
- Lack of empathy
- Insomnia
- Asthma
- Upper back pain
- Weak immune system
- Issues with the blood circulation
- Chest pain
- Angina
- Breasts, lungs, and heart issues

Throat Chakra

Location: The throat

Sanskrit Name: Visuddha chakra

Color: Blue

Sound: Ham

Functions: Being yourself and speaking your truth are feelings associated with an open throat chakra. As the "throat" chakra, it rules over voice and communication skills. You can healthily express yourself, speak up, and truly listen to others. This chakra is also responsible for inspiring. It supplies energy to the neck, hands, shoulder, arms, parathyroid, and thyroid glands.

Symptoms of a Blocked Throat Chakra

- Shyness
- Inability to express your feelings
- Difficulty speaking up
- Aggressive behavior
- Do you feel misunderstood?
- Difficulty paying attention
- Feeling unfocused
- Worrying about what others think of you
- Sore throat

- Headaches
- Stiffness and tension in the shoulders and neck
- Thyroid difficulties

Third Eye Chakra

Location: Center of the forehead

Sanskrit Name: Ajna chakra

Color: Indigo

Sound: Aum

Functions: The third eye chakra rules over intuition. This chakra acts as a bridge between yourself and the world around you. It can also be a focal point when practicing yoga to help you remain focused and aware. When open, this chakra removes a "veil" from over our eyes that is clouding our judgment so that we can see the bigger picture. It is also connected to self-knowledge, intelligence, and insight. The third eye chakra is responsible for neurological functions, the pituitary gland, and vision.

Symptoms of a Blocked Third Eye Chakra

- Greed and only caring about material things
- Lack of purpose
- Self-doubt
- Feeling disconnected from our truest selves
- Impatience
- Depression • Feeling consumed with negative thoughts
- Narrow mindedness
- Feeling burdened with the past
- Confusion
- Lack of concentration
- Indecisiveness
- Feeling unassertive
- Fear of success
- Huge ego
- Denial
- Memory issues

- Difficulty accessing the intuition
- Inability to learn new skills
- Difficulty trusting and listening to your inner voice
- Feeling judgmental
- Feeling overwhelmed
- Anxiety and depression
- Migraines and headaches
- Dizziness
- Insomnia
- Blurry vision
- Endocrine imbalance
- Brain disorders
- Exhaustion

Crown Chakra

Location: Crown) of the head

Sanskrit Name: Sahastrara chakra

Color: Violet or white

Sound: Silence (we listen instead of chanting)

Functions: The crown chakra is the last of the seven chakras, and it rules over our spiritual connection to the divine and our higher selves. It is also considered the center of enlightenment. When open, it elevates our consciousness and makes us feel at one with the universe and connected to all its beings. As a result of being connected to the universe and the divine, we experience wisdom, self-realization, and enlightenment. It gives you a purpose in life, increases your awareness, and makes you see there is more to life than the pursuit of worldly things. The crown chakra is responsible for the central nervous system, pituitary gland, and cerebral cortex.

Symptoms of a Blocked Crown Chakra

- Sadness
- Frustration
- Destructive feelings
- Lack of inspiration

- Lacking a sense of purpose
- Apathy
- Depression
- Disconnection from the universe and all its beings
- Spiritual cynicism
- Lack of energy
- Trouble sleeping (desire to sleep all day)
- Headaches and migraines
- Exhaustion
- Destructive behavior

Exercises

Now that you have learned about the chakras, we will provide simple exercises to help you open each one.

The Root Chakra

This exercise will help you feel safe and grounded.

- Stand barefoot on the floor or grass, or sit leaning your back against a wall or a tree
- Repeat to yourself out loud, "I am safe."

The Sacral Chakra

- Find a private, quiet, and safe space
- Allow yourself to feel whatever you truly feel at this very moment. Do whatever feels right, like singing, crying, laughing, dancing, jumping, or screaming

The Solar Plexus Chakra

One of the best exercises for this chakra is to see the glass half full by looking at the brighter side of life. This will allow you to eliminate negative emotions and thoughts and replace them with positive ones.

- Buy a gratitude journal or download a gratitude journal app on your phone
- Write down one or more things or more that you are grateful for every day

This exercise will open your eyes to all the good things in your life, improving your mental health and well-being.

The Heart Chakra

To open this chakra, you need to give and receive love. This can be done by practicing visualization.

- Sit in a relaxing position in a quiet place
- Close your eyes
- Imagine someone you truly love and tell them, "they deserve to be loved and happy."
- Now imagine someone you are mad at, and tell them the same thing
- Lastly, imagine you are also telling yourself you deserve to be loved

The Throat Chakra

To open this chakra, you should speak your truth and express yourself. Focus on finding your voice and clearly communicating your thoughts. You can do this gradually and in one-on-one situations first. Start with the people closest to you and whom you are comfortable around until you are ready to express yourself to more people. If you need to speak your truth, do it. Train yourself never to stay silent when you have something to say unless it is inappropriate or you are angry (when it is better to remain silent!)

The Third Eye Chakra

The best exercise for this chakra is candle-gazing meditation.

- Sit in a dark and quiet room
- Light a candle
- Gaze at the candle while breathing deeply for a few minutes
- Close your eyes so they can adjust. Then when you are ready, open them and go on with your day

The Crown Chakra

This chakra is about finding your purpose in life and increasing your self-awareness. The best exercise here is to get to know yourself better. Through journaling, ask yourself questions and answer them. You can also download an app with interesting questions that will help you learn so much about yourself.

Learning everything about the subtle bodies and chakras will pave the way to mastering and manipulating energy. Take your time and practice the exercises we have mentioned daily to help you advance as a practitioner.

Chapter 3: Meditation and Visualization

Part-I: MEDITATION

What Is Meditation?

Meditation is the art of calming the mind. It is used to promote relaxation, build inner strength, and is the art of concentrating on a single object or point. It involves sitting quietly, focusing on your breath, and reciting a mantra or prayer.

Meditation and visualization.
https://pixabay.com/es/photos/meditar-lago-estado-animico-4882027/

Meditation helps slow down our minds because they work 24/7, and thoughts keep racing through our minds. Thoughts can be about important issues or could be you overthinking things and disturbing your internal peace. Meditation can be practiced at any time in a peaceful environment to focus and relax.

Different Types of Meditation

There are many different kinds of meditation techniques performed worldwide, and you are bound to find one which resonates with you and your needs. The point of meditation is to reach mental peace and physical relaxation.

1. Guided Meditation

This is the type of meditation performed to achieve certain things. It can be your work achievement, weight, peace, or health. In this mediation, we focus and visualize imagery of what we want to achieve. Guided meditation also helps get rid of mental blocks to see the clarity of things.

2. Tartak Meditation

This technique helps to focus on things. This type of meditation is performed when we want to focus on work but can't – due to distractions. In this style of meditation, we focus on one point, place, or candle flame as long as possible to improve our concentration level.

3. Transcended Meditation

This meditation is where a word, sound, or phrase is repeated or received until your mind transcends into a different world.

4. Mindfulness Meditation

Mindfulness meditation is adopted from Buddhist meditation. In this, we focus on present moments and on inhales and exhales of breathing. It is a simple meditative technique, and anyone can do it quite easily.

A Simple Method to Meditate

There are many techniques to meditation, but if we look at a simple meditation practice, we can not go wrong with mindfulness meditation. Root yourself in the present, and pay attention to what is around you.

To perform this meditation, we must follow some basic and simple steps.

1. The first thing that you need to do is to find a comfortable position. Finding a peaceful and comfortable position to perform this meditation is wise because distraction can ruin the purpose of this meditation. But it is not necessary to find a place outside your house. You can do it in your room, office, or any other quiet and peaceful place.

2. Many yogis recommend performing the meditation in a certain leg and hand position at a certain angle, but it is simple meditation, and for beginners as well, so it does not matter which leg position you are following. You must cross your legs comfortably and put your hands on your knees or lap.

3. Keep your back straight during meditation. However, if you suffer from injury or pain or have just started your meditation journey, you can place a pillow on your back or lean against the wall.

4. The fourth step is to close your eyes and focus on one thing. Breathe in and out, focusing on your breathing. Experience your chest moving in and out. While doing this, feel your chest, shoulder, belly, or anything that feels appropriate. It is okay to have thoughts while meditating, but one should struggle to overcome those distractions to better focus.

5. Ideally, it is recommended to meditate for at least 20 minutes a day. However, if you are a beginner, you can meditate for a few minutes, set a timer, and see how much time you can meditate in a day. Increase the time by one minute a day until you reach the recommended 20 -30 minutes.

Mindfulness meditation also helps in spiritual awakening, so keep a positive mindset and be patient during meditation.

Master the Breathing Technique

When practicing meditation, especially mindfulness meditation, it is important to focus on your breath.

To master the breathing techniques during meditation, you first need to sit straight and firmly on the ground. The position of your knees and hips should be at a 90-degree angle, and your back should be straight. However, if you have an injury or are experiencing pain, you can lean on the wall or support your back with a pillow or cushion.

Start by taking deep, natural breaths without altering or controlling them. After taking a breath at a natural rhythm, take a deep breath through the nose and feel that breath into your body.

Feel the expanding and contraction of the lungs as you inhale and exhale, and feel the breath in your belly and other body parts. Take another deep breath and repeat the process a few times.

Now take a deep breath from your nose and exhale through your month.

When you take a deep breath from your nose, you'll feel a warm sensation of air on the upper mouth area and coolness when it releases.

Continue the process of warmness and coolness of the air in your nostrils for a few minutes. After completion, bring back your attention slowly and gently open your eyes.

Several Benefits of Meditation

Meditation helps you slow down the number of thoughts that are affecting your mental health and physical capabilities. Meditation increases positive emotions and helps to control emotions like anger or grief. It helps to increase the ability to focus and concentrate.

Deep breathing during meditation helps stay clear, strengthening the immune system. It helps to cure depression and also helps in spiritual awakening. It also decreases anxiety, stress, and pain.

1. A Gateway to Psychic Energy

Meditation is a powerful tool that helps to grow psychic capabilities. Everyone can develop psychic abilities through meditation.

When we meditate, we clear our minds and focus more on our breathing. Meditation gives you a heightened awareness and helps you connect to your center and create energy inside your body.

Many people take meditation as a tool, a primary purpose for relaxation and de-stress, and focusing more, but that is all a by-product of meditation. Meditation helps you get rid of anger, greed, and delusion. When we meditate, we get rid of all things, creating internal energy in us to go on a path of spiritual enlightenment.

2. Make Energy Healing (Reiki) Possible

Defined in simple terms, Reiki is universal energy we get through meditation. It is a Japanese style of channeling energy through the whole body. This energy gives immersive relief and also helps to connect with spirit guides. Spirit guides only connect and communicate with humans if they have high energy and frequency, and Reiki helps to develop that energy.

Reiki meditation is performed by sitting in a quiet place with a specific position of hands at specific points on the body. It helps cure depression and anxiety and brings more focus and a calm mind.

3. The Gassho Prayer

Dr. Mikao Usui created the Gassho prayer technique, and the prayer word translates as: "two hands coming together."

To perform Gassho's prayer, you need to sit calmly with a straight back and closed eyes and sit in the position just as we do in meditation. Position your hands in the prayer position placing the hands and palms together in the "Namaste" position in front of the hand chakra.

If you are distracted by something, you could press your middle fingertips gently to refocus attention and get rid of thoughts.

Take deep breaths and do this for 15-30 minutes. You can start with five minutes daily if you are just a beginner. This helps you focus more, purifies your mind and heart, and brings out positivity.

Part-II: VISUALIZATION

What Is Visualization?

Visualization is a technique that focuses and calms the mind while also promoting creativity and problem-solving skills. Visualization is a thought process. We think about something first in our mind – and then manifest it into the physical plane.

The goal of visualization is to create images in the mind that are positive and relaxing, to achieve a state of relaxation and focus, and help to move energy within the body.

Five Techniques to Visualize

While it may take a while before you get accustomed to this process, there are five basic techniques to get started with visualization.

Technique # 1. Color Breathing

This type of visualization helps relieve stress and brings positive vibes and a good mood.

1. For this, you need to consider a color you like.
2. Sit in a comfortable position, just as you do in meditation. Now, close your eyes and take deep breaths, placing all of your attention on your breathing.
3. Then, visualize the color you have chosen. Choose the color you may be feeling right now or one which will give you soothing vibes.

4. Take deep breaths while holding that color in your mind. Imagine breathing and spreading this color throughout your body in the form of light into all parts of your body. If, at any time, thoughts, images, or sounds come to mind during visualization, acknowledge them and gently ignore them.

5. When you breathe out, visualize that you are breathing out stress and worries

Continue this visualization and breathing process as long as you want to lighten the relevant body part.

Technique # 2. Compassion Meditation Visualization

Compassion Meditation helps you to understand the suffering of others and their feelings and to feel love for them. Compassion Meditation visualization leads to improved moods, good behavior, and less anger and greed. Below are the steps to follow:

1. To start, get yourself comfortable. Close your eyes and breathe in and out, feeling yourself breathe. Take deep breaths in natural places without forcing yourself.

2. Then visualize the person you want to send love, grief, and compassion to. It can be a loved one or your own pets or animals.

3. Picture them in your thoughts and think about how you feel about them, whether you have a love for them or want to be compassionate to them in their pain. Be deliberate and true about the feeling you want to send. Imagine the feeling in your mind, and surround that feeling with a golden light.

4. Use these words: "The pain is going; the peace is coming." Remember to breathe as you chant this. Focus on the golden feeling you imagined and see it leaving your body. It is traveling to the person who needs it. You can also retain the golden feeling if you need the healing.

5. After completing this, you'll fill love and freedom from pain. Repeat this visualization as needed.

Technique # 3. Progressive Muscle Relaxation

This muscle visualization exercise helps you release muscle tension and stiffness due to anxiety or stress. Below are the exact steps to follow:

1. Find a comfortable position.

2. Take a slow deep breath through your nostrils, and hold it for a few seconds.

3. Again, take a deep breath, close your eyes, and tighten your forehand and mouth muscles. After five seconds, exhale it while visualizing the tension leaving your body.

4. Again, take a deep breath while squeezing the muscles of your hands for five minutes. Imagine you are squeezing a lemon for lemonade.

5. Exhale and visualize that all the tension is released from your body as exhaling the air out.

6. Take a slow, deep breath again while squeezing the shoulder muscles for five seconds, and try to touch your ears with your shoulder.

7. Repeat the same inhalation and exhalation process in all of your muscles

Technique # 4. Guided Imagery

Guided imagery helps you to release stress and cure depression by visualizing images, scenery, and positive pictures.

1. For this, sit comfortably and close your eyes, just as in meditation.

2. Inhale deeply and visualize the scenery or images with each breath.

3. When you want to exhale, visualize the stress, unmanageable feelings, and anxiety leaving your body

Technique # 5. Goals visualization

The technique of goals visualization is used to imagine your goals or secure your future. In this meditation, visualize their future or goals and create a scene in imagination.

1. Visualize your success. See your goal in your mind in great detail, and see yourself achieving it.

2. If some negative thoughts appear, recite the mantra and keep faith in yourself.

3. Take a slow, deep breath, exhale, and visualize your success or goals.

With these techniques, you can explore the realm of visualization and find the one that suits you best.

Habits to Promote Visualization

1. Avoiding the Habit of Overthinking

To practice visualization, it is important not to overthink. During meditation and visualization, distractions occur.

For instance, in visualization, if you are practicing color breathing or image visualization and want to focus on one box or color, your brain might start to overthink the shape of the box or which color to choose, etc. This type of distraction ruins the purpose of visualization.

However, it is normal to overthink, and you can slowly overcome it by practicing visualization regularly.

2. Using All Your Senses

Use all of your scenes to get more benefit from visualization. For example, try to use all senses if you imagine some scenery or image. Try to feel, smell, and use your body in that scenario. It will boost the visualization, and you'll benefit from it.

3. Parting Ways with Judgements

In visualization, it is important not to judge or compare yourself to others. The mind is a chatterbox, and it keeps thinking round the clock, which is quite exhausting.

Many necessary or unusual thoughts appear in your mind. For instance, during visualization, you suddenly start to think about your to-do list or upcoming work instead of visualizing. Try not to judge yourself because everything takes time, and you can focus more on visualization if you practice daily.

4. Stay Relaxed While Practicing

The foremost step in visualization is to relax, sit in a comfortable position, and have a peaceful environment that calms your mind. Practice visualization daily. Start with five minutes each day and then increase the period by one minute daily.

Various Benefits of Visualization

There are many overlapping advantages of meditation and visualization, leading to some people becoming confused between the two. Visualization has some distinct benefits that highlight its significance and positive impact. Below are some of its benefits:

1. It helps in reducing stress and enhances focus and clarity. In short, it optimizes the overall functioning of your senses. In this manner, it is a great tool for artists or writers.

2. Visualization also provides great emotional stability and may even promote the spirit of kindness.

3. Once you start practicing "visualization," you'll notice a substantial improvement in your sleep quality and boost your immune system.

4. In addition, it helps bring positive energy to the body. It also enhances creativity and builds problem-solving skills.

That said, meditation and visualization go hand in hand, and you cannot separate the two if you truly want to experience a deep positive impact.

Chapter 4: Working with Your Guides

Spirit guides are the universal forces that help protect, love, and guide us towards wisdom. They are our companions and our divine parents. They are with us before we are even born and can take any form.

The way spirit guides appear or present themselves to us is based on what we believe. They can be in the form of Angels, Animals, Ancestors, Ancients, plants, or any form that has significance to you. Spirit guides are here to help us. Their main purpose is to teach or comfort us, but they also help us learn about ourselves and show us the right path to grow.

Different Types of Spirit Guides

There are many types of spirit guides, and we have listed a few below, together with a brief description.

1. Angel Spirit Guides

Guardian angels are here to teach us valuable lessons, guide us through our hardships, and help us differentiate between right and wrong.

They are non-denominational; subsequently, they protect and guide people of all beliefs and faiths. We all have more than one Guardian Angel. They are known as the "awakened ones," and if we call them spiritually, they will guide us.

2. Animal Spirit Guides

Animals are well-known powerful spirit guides. They are raw and pure. Sometimes, they are pets who have passed on and come back to aid you.

We can also have spiritual guidance through animals around us. For example, bears teach us how to be strong and confident, butterflies show us how we can change ourselves into a better people, cats show us how to be independent, and dogs teach us how to stay loyal and show unconditional love to our loved ones, and owls show us wisdom.

Butterflies are an example of animal spirit guides.
https://pixabay.com/es/photos/mariposas-flores-polinizar-1127666/

We can take spiritual guidance from animals around us by spending time outside and focusing on the unusual behavior of animals which sometimes appear, again and again, paying attention to every activity around us. They teach us the lesson of empowerment, how to let go of small things, and lessons of love and joy.

3. Ancestors as Spirit Guides

Departed loved ones can also be your spirit guides. They can support you from heaven and show you the right path, whether your career path or life journey.

They can be anyone, whether you have a blood connection with them or not. Any human who passes can become your spirit guide who was once in the same position as yours and now wants to help you out from that.

4. Masters as Spirit Guides

Masters like Buddha are the ultimate teachers. They are enlightened ones and give guidance and teach us during the journey of spiritual awakening. They work as leaders or teachers in the spirit world and help us connect with the divine.

5. Protection Spirit Guides

Protection spirit guides or helper angels help humans in their difficulties. They give signals and signs to warn humans about dangerous situations they might face in the future. They protect and help them in their daily chores.

6. Light Beings

This is another name for a guardian angel, but people don't always like to use the term angel. They are spirits who help guide people through difficult situations or recover from traumatic events. They will likely be shrouded in light to both literally and metaphorically guide you down the right path.

How to Work with Spirit Guides

Spirit guides, our guardians, and our protectors are easy to connect and communicate with, but you should have inner belief in them. They can not interfere in your life until you ask them.

Spirit guide helpers or angels exist on higher frequency levels, and we can not necessarily see them with our physical eyes. Yet, they can communicate with us through symbols and signs and establish connections to yourself and your heart.

To visualize yourself with the spirit guides, you must imagine yourself at a higher frequency and energy level. Once you are at an aligned frequency, the spirit guides will respond to your call. However, if you are unable to tune into their energy levels, your spirit guide will not be able to hear your message.

The average frequency level of a human being is 62 to 75 MHz, and if you are feeling unwell, you'll notice your frequency level will fall below 62MHz. The higher the frequency level, the higher the chances they can hear you.

All divine angels help and guide us, but you need to be alert to their signals which can sometimes be very subtle. A spirit guide will find ways to communicate; it is a human's job to listen to them.

Everyone has angels – a team of spirit guides ready to help when asked. Try to interpret their message, create a language, a way to communicate with them because they will find ways to help you, but one should be able to tune into their intuition.

A Simple Way to Connect with Them

Spiritual guides speak in silence, or they give us signals and signs. The signs might be a physical sign or message.

Keep your mind conscious but separate it from the outside world to connect with them. The mind is super active. It keeps thinking of things, upcoming works, and many other life problems. The more thoughts in your mind, the less it can listen and focus on spirit guides.

The mind works like a filter that separates the outside world and illusion. You must keep your mind conscious and try to communicate with your spiritual guide.

Practice the Art of Meditation

Meditation helps connect spirit guides.
https://www.pexels.com/photo/fashion-people-woman-relaxation-8391315/

Meditation can help to connect with them through the conscious mind. It generates internal peace and lets you keep worries and problems out of your mind so you can easily communicate with your spirit's guides.

To meditate, find a nice, calm, and peaceful environment where no outside source or voice can disturb you. Try to calm your body, sit comfortably with closed eyes, and play mantras or prayers for five to ten minutes.

Through this conscious period, you'll feel many things. Set a goal of two to three weeks, as you probably will not feel something right away because spiritual guidance depends upon the energy and belief level.

There is another level of consciousness that is the heart.

When you can connect with your spirit guides easily, you'll see *after that time* that you'll not receive any signals or signs – and you do not need to call your spirit guides to help you. Instead, your heart is giving signals, telling you what is right and wrong or which path is best for you. This happens because you have reached a higher level of spiritual awakening, and Angel, or master or spirit guide, is within you.

Another important part of connecting with your guides is allowing them to help you out in your life. You can allow them into your life by permitting them. Permit them aloud or in your heart. You can also write a note in a journal.

After allowing them, ask them for message reinforcement, ask them to reinforce the message into 3D reality, physical signs, and messages.

The quieter your mind is, the easier it will be to connect with your spirit guides. Stay present, keep your mind conscious in looking at and observing the outside world, and don't miss the messages. Sometimes, spirit guides give message signals repeatedly, but your mind doesn't receive them because it is not paying attention to the messages. Make sure to keep your mind conscious after asking for help.

Spirit guides can also appear in your dreams. Before going to bed, relax and ask them to appear in dreams or send you signals in your dreams. Again, they will not instantly appear, but try again and again and put maximum energy and consciousness into asking.

You can also connect with them through tarots. You can read tarots on your own or get someone to read them for you. Playing soothing music and exercising will also help you connect with spirit guides.

Signs That They Are Communicating

Spirit guides communicate with us in subtle ways to help us in certain aspects of life. They can send us signs in many ways, and it is up to us how much we are spiritually awakened to understand them.

1. Vivid Dreams

Spirit guides sometimes create vivid scenarios and convey their messages through dreams and visions. However, it can happen that when you wake up, you completely forget the dream, so to remember it, write down as much as you remember in a journal and try to focus on which signal your spirit guide has given to you.

2. Intuition

Spirit guides often send us messages through intuition. We can hear strong telephonic voices or strong gut feelings for certain kinds of work or people.

These signals are for spirit guides to help and guide you from difficult situations.

3. Music

Music is a universal language with a higher frequency level that helps spirit guides to communicate with us.

If you suddenly saw or heard some old music or lyrics that have some connections with your life, then it might be a signal from spirit guides.

4. Repeated Numbers

If you see repeated numbers, quotes, or phrases, then your spirit guides could be trying to connect with you through written materials and give a message repeatedly.

5. Touch

If you feel any light-weight touches on your neck, shoulders, or head and a sensation that someone is either there accompanying or watching you, then you do not need to be afraid because spiritual guides are providing you consultation.

Other signs include smell, a sudden nice and pleasant smell that reminds you of your past or any important event.

White feathers are also a sign from spiritual guides. It indicates the sign of luck. It can be found in the strangest places that you might not accept, but if you see white feathers, consider it a sign from your spirit guides.

Benefits of Having Spirit Guides

Spirit guides are positive incorporeal entities that guide and offer assistance to living human beings. And by connecting with them, you can connect between two different worlds, the materialistic one and the spiritual one.

1. Guidance

Spirit Guides are guardians of the soul. They provide us with the right path and help us in our life's ups and downs. They will guide us through our whole life span.

One should have faith in their spirit guide and thank them after guidance.

2. Support

They are a support system. By connecting with them, you'll never feel alone. They will be with you in any obstacles and guide and support you.

They are navigators of life and can help us in our relationship or friendship issues and career path and protect us from making wrong decisions.

3. Master

They become masters or mentors of our life once we connect with them. Spirit guides are the best companions and best friends of human beings.

They help you deal with the outside world, and by having their friendship on your side, you can easily face any hurdles in your life because they mentor and teach you in every phase of life.

4. Protections

They protect every aspect of life and from any bad things. To protect ourselves from bad things, we should focus on things happening around us because guidance continuously gives signals to us.

If you do not feel good intentions from something or someone, stay away from that because it might be a signal from Spirit guides.

How Do They Complement a Psychic Reiki Session?

Reiki guides the universal energy that is in all of us. In this process, therapists can channel energy into patients' bodies to activate natural healing and spiritual awakening.

Reiki is performed to ease pain and depression, and relaxation of one's body and helps to filter out the mind from unusual thoughts.

To connect with your spirit guides, it is essential to call them by using energy and a higher frequency. The higher the energy level, the sooner they will respond. But sudden blockage will affect upon calling them, and Reiki is often performed to remove the sudden blockage from the body.

Reiki is often performed by placing hands in specific positions. You might feel sudden pressure on the chest and tingling in your arms and legs during this. This sensation indicates the blockage of energy. During Reiki, the body will release stress and depression and return to its natural state.

Sudden pressure and tingling signify that your body is reaching its natural state and removing its blockage.

Reiki transfers positive energy to patients so they can focus more on current events. Reiki clarifies the mind and helps you concentrate on the problems and opportunities in your life. By focusing on current events, you'll likely catch a sign or message from Spiritual Gods.

Reiki helps in sleeping better. After a reiki session, your body will feel completely relaxed and tension-free, which will help you sleep and heal better, and a peaceful sleep means more chances of vivid dreams that give you signs and guide you.

Helps with Harmony and Balance

Reiki moves the energy around your body, unblocking blockages and sending the energy where it needs to go—creating balance. This includes all of the body systems and creates an environment of harmony conducive to a balanced lifestyle.

Reiki helps you with physical relaxation. It helps your body to go into its natural state. It helps you focus on whatever you are trying to put your energy into.

Reiki originated in Japan in 2000 and was later introduced around the globe. As it moved further around the world, the art was further developed. Reiki is not only hand movement but can be a pet therapy, music, deep breathing, and much more. All of this therapy can be a meditative spiritual awakening.

A Reiki session is performed to calm the mind and help in spiritual awakening.

In reiki sessions, besides hand massage, music is often used to relax your mind. This therapy is called Karuna therapy. During this therapy, therapists play soothing music, a record of nature, and audio sounds to transmit energy and positive messages in your body.

Another psychic reiki session includes rainbow Reiki. In this session, seven main chakras in the body are used to bring healing. This spiritual bringing is used to heal and understand the nature and things around us.

Aromatic reiki sessions also help in spiritual awakening. A reiki session combined with aromatherapy oils is a great relaxer and also brings pleasure. Aromatherapy oils have strong scents that link to the person, their past life, or any special events. Through this, the person can be focused more on past events and focus on spiritual guides.

Many ways and many other types of Reiki complement and initiate the spiritual awakening of human beings.

Chapter 5: Clearing and Grounding

The world around us is wired with energy, both good and bad. The people we interact with and the tools or objects we use daily have energy fields and auras. What you may not notice is that these things have a significant impact on our own energies, as strong vibrations can easily attract us toward them. This is why regular energy clearing is essential. It allows us to identify our own vibrational frequency and guarantee that our inner aura flows smoothly.

Energy clearing can help us eliminate intrusive thoughts and emotions, allowing us to maintain a positive outlook on life. Since energy is supposed to flow, attempting to suppress the negativity or push it to the back of our minds only creates added problems. Clearing can allow you to let unhelpful vibrations flow outside the mind and body. This practice's effects are not experienced immediately but are felt gradually. The more you practice the techniques, the more you'll get the hang of it. It requires a lot of determination, focus, and, most importantly, patience.

Picture the world itself as one enormous battery. It is naturally charged with its own unique, subtle energy. It ensures our stability, protection, and safety. Everything electrical, whether it is a television or our bodies, is connected to the Earth. This is what we know as being "grounded." Practicing grounding can help diminish stress and tension and promote positive energies like strength and balance. We feel centered when we are grounded and experience fewer physical pain and symptoms.

The physical symptoms we experience are not as upfront as we think. Let us take headaches, for example. Most people do not think much of this seemingly min0r ailment. They take a pain reliever and call it a day. However, what they do not realize is that their physical condition can be a manifestation of a hindrance in their energetic flow. Headaches could be a sign of stress, uncertainty, a lack of mental clarity, an abundance of negative thoughts, and more. This is why headaches usually accompany the compelling need to just step away from everything. We should never ignore our physical symptoms because, in most cases, our bodies are trying to tell us something. Indulging in a stress-relieving activity or practicing a hobby can help you raise your vibrations and release the accumulated negative energies.

Any type of healing work must be preceded by energy clearing and grounding. In this chapter, we will explain what clearing and grounding are. We will also review some techniques you can use to cleanse your energy and center yourself.

What Is Energy Clearing?

Many confuse "energy healing" and "energy clearing." While it may sound like both of them refer to the same process, the concepts are very different. You can not start the healing process unless you have cleared your energy. Healing your energy is concerned with all types of imbalances. After all, energy is the foundation of everything. Even intangibles, such as emotions, thoughts, and our spiritual side, are all energy. Energy clearing, on the other hand, refers to certain situations. Sometimes, you'll find yourself someplace or dealing with something with an energy that no longer serves you. In that case, you would take remedial action, energy clearing, to release these negative energies.

Do I Need to Clear My Energy?

Anyone with a blockage in their vibrational energy needs to practice energy clearing activities. But how can you work out if you need to clear your energy?

The following are some telltale signs that your energy needs to be cleared:

- You struggle with insomnia, poor quality of sleep, or other sleep problems.

- You are drained, depressed, stressed, anxious, or lethargic for no apparent reason.

- You are always fatigued even after sleeping well through the night.

- You are suddenly experiencing a wide range of health problems, whether simultaneously or one after the other. Examples include physical pain, muscle tension, stiffness, headaches, lethargy, dizziness, etc.

- You always sense negativity in the air. There is a constant feeling that something bad is happening or going to happen.

- Something feels off, but you just can not lay a finger on what the problem may be.

- You can not shake negative feelings, vibes, or impressions regarding a place, situation, or person.

- You can not sit or stand still, especially if this is atypical behavior. You're always restless or fidgeting around.

- You are in stagnant energy, or you feel stuck.

- Your emotions are all over the place, or you experience extreme shifts or sudden hits of emotions without clear or compelling reasons.

- You are unproductive, unable to control your thoughts, experiencing brain fog, or your mind and actions are going in circles.

- You need to clear your energy if you notice that your energy is off and you cannot pinpoint what is causing the problem.

Clearing Energies

Bubble of Light

The "Bubble of Light" technique is among the most popular energy clearing practices, primarily because it is easy and effective. This method can be practiced while standing up, sitting, or lying down.

Get into a comfortable position and close your eyes. Focus on your center. Imagine that there is a small, harmless flame there. The flame is white, and as you dwell on it, it becomes brighter and stronger. You are going to ask this flame to protect your body. It is going to stop outside influences from damaging you. Visualize the gradual growth of this flame until it lights up your entire body. Once you see that this light has filled you, urge it to penetrate your skin, making its way to your energy body.

This practice can be done daily or when you feel you need it. It can come in handy when there is plenty of energy in the air. Excuse yourself from overwhelming family gatherings, vehement meetings, arguments, or other unpleasant interactions to complete this practice. If that is not possible, doing it afterward can help you release unwanted energies.

Namaste Hands

The chances are that you have heard of the popular yoga practice where the practitioners bring their hands together and say "namaste." It is perhaps the most common Hindu and Buddhist valediction. What you may not know, however, is that this practice holds a much deeper meaning.

When you think about it, the essence of yoga is to clear and restructure the energy and space within the physical, spiritual, emotional, and mental aspects of your being. After the time and effort you have dedicated to letting go of what no longer serves you to make the space for positivity, you can create a symbolic circle to close in these efforts by bringing your hands together. Placing your flat palms parallel to your heart helps you confirm that what you have released remains outside your body, and everything you have attracted and built stays safely inside. While it is ideally practiced after another healing or clearing activity, you can reap its benefits by doing it at any time and place. However, bringing your hands together in front of your arms in a public setting would seem weird. Sitting at a table, you can do it under its surface. The heart plays a significant symbolic role. But the hand and touch are more powerful. Doing it whenever there is a lot of undesired energy hanging around allows you to declare that nothing will go in or go out without your permission. Our palms have receptive and expressive centers that serve as barriers.

Cording

Cording is an age-old practice that is influenced by shamanic practices. Ironically, this technique feels a lot like a de-cording practice that clears the energy and protects and contains it. Cords refer to energetic bonds and connections that an individual cultivates with another person, a group of people, a place, a habit, an idea, an emotional wound, or even an object. It is called a cord because it is not just a connection but a vehicle that enables energy exchange between both entities. The energy given or received is not always equally reciprocated. In toxic relationships, your energy is drained and never replenished.

As we have just explained, a cord is formed when you build a connection with another entity. Cords can also be formed if another person attaches them to you, even when you do not attempt to forge the same connection. A teacher does so with their students, and authors do that with readers. These cords can either be attached maliciously due to hatred, disgust, or jealousy or positively as a reflection of admiration and respect. Either way, these cords are out of your scope of control, leaving you unable to control your own energy. For instance, people who can not get over their past relationships usually try to re-cultivate these cords. More often than not, this creates a harmful effect. The best way to remedy this situation would be by practicing this technique.

Start with the Mountain Pose and slowly allow your eyes to shut. See the energy flowing through your body—it is all connected. Move from the top of your head to the tips of your toes. As you do so, imagine yourself plucking these cords and releasing them from your body. Go over your energy body, plucking all the cords three times. Then, end your practice with the "Bubble of Light" exercise.

Reiji Ho

Reiji Ho is a Reiki energy clearing technique. Unlike other standard Reiki hand poses, this particular method is more intuitive. It helps its practitioners locate imbalances and encourage balance, creating energetic healing opportunities.

To practice this technique, sit comfortably and bring your hands to Gassho, or prayer position. Close your eyes and bring your attention to the hard center in your lower belly or abdomen. Stay focused on your breathing. Activate Reiki, allowing its energy to flow throughout your entire body, making its way to all of your cells. Envision it filling you up and the space around you.

Move your hands to your forehead, requesting holistic healing. Do not guide your hands, but let them make their way toward the areas in your body that need healing. Do not supervise the process nor disrupt it. Where your hands stop, allow them to pass on the positive energies. You can intuitively tell when you have finished a certain area or the entire process. When you are done, rest your palms on your lap. Take a few breaths and acknowledge your gratitude.

How to Clear the Energy

Smudging

Smudging is a very effective energy clearing technique. It is known to have various health benefits due to its antimicrobial qualities. It is also proven to positively influence the mood and aid with insomnia.

Keep a door or window open as you practice this technique. This serves as a safety measure and a gateway for negative energies to leave your space. Start by setting your intentions regarding the things you wish to release and cleanse your space. Come up with a relevant prayer or mantra you can repeat throughout the process. A simple mantra would be, "I let go of what doesn't serve me." Now that you are ready, hold the sage at approximately a 45-degree angle and light it using a candle or match. Allow it to burn for 20 seconds before blowing out the flame. You should see orange embers before the smoke billows upward. Walk slowly around the space to spread the smoke around, gently guiding it and the negative energy toward the door or window. To extinguish the sage, press it firmly onto a fireproof surface.

Use a Singing Bowl

Sounds, especially bells, can absorb negative energies and drive them away. Singing bowls have pure, bell-like, resonating tones that can help energy levels fall into balance. To use this instrument, you need to position it gently onto the palm of your hands. Bring your awareness to how it feels and its weight on your hands. When you are ready, strike the rim of the bowl gently a couple of times to familiarize yourself with its sound. Start playing it freely, allowing the energies to flow into your body. Move around, so it fills up your space. In each place you go, strike it three times, and bring your awareness to the tone that it makes. Some places will cause a dull sound, while others will allow for the generation of more lively sounds, reflecting the energies in different places. Focus on ringing the bowl near walls, windows, and doors. You can move the mallet in a clockwise circle over the rim as an alternative to striking the bowl.

What Is Grounding?

Grounding is a therapeutic practice that is alternatively known as "earthing." Practicing this technique requires you to ground yourself and cultivate a strong electrical connection with the earth. Grounding physics and earthing science are scientific fields concerned with how electric charges from the Earth can positively influence one's body. It is very important to note that the grounding techniques used to aid in coping with mental health issues are different from these types of grounding techniques.

Anyone can practice grounding techniques. They are very beneficial when it comes to tuning and balancing the physical and spiritual energies in our being. Grounding allows you to shift your consciousness to the present, physical moment. This promotes a steady and centered energy, making you more focused and mentally stronger.

How to Ground Yourself

Tree Root

Go out in nature and find a safe, quiet space to stand or sit barefoot on the ground. Keep your feet flat on the ground and take deep breaths, focusing on how the earth feels underneath you. Visualize your feet growing roots that make their way to Earth's center. Breathe in deeply from the roots, pulling the energy through your soles and into your body. Allow it to traverse your being, nourishing you in the process. Imagine the stress making its way out of the crown of your head. Raise your arms and visualize them as long tree branches. Reach up to feel the warmth of the sun. Feed off the relaxing energies of the sun and earth.

Use Healing Crystals

Wear or carry with you a healing crystal to ground yourself. Bear in mind that each healing crystal serves a different purpose. Choose carnelian, bloodstone, gold tiger eye, hematite, amber, pyrite, or garnet when it comes to grounding.

Earthing

Take a walk barefoot on sand, grass, or dirt. This will help you reinvigorate your energy.

You can think of energy as a spectrum with a light end and a very dark one. Compassion, care, love, and other positive vibrations fall into the light side of the spectrum. Hatred, fear, and similar low and negative vibrations lie on the dark side of the spectrum. Everything in the world, including humans and inanimate objects, constantly sends out and receives energy. This is why we must reflect on our daily life and interactions to monitor these energy exchanges before we embark on the healing journey.

Chapter 6: Developing Your Psychic Abilities

Have you ever wondered how tarot and oracle readers gather all the information they need to give their clients a better understanding of their reality and insights into what is in store for them? The key here is nothing more than the four clairs of intuition. Psychics and readers constantly work on developing and strengthening their intuition. When you are highly intuitive, you can easily grasp what is trying to be communicated to you. The four clairs are known as clairaudience, which means "clear hearing," clairvoyance, meaning "clear seeing," clairsentience refers to "clear feelings," and claircognizance, which is "clear knowing."

Some people are born with naturally stronger clairs. It is not uncommon to find someone who has very strong clairsentience but weak clairvoyant abilities. There are many online quizzes you can take to discover your strongest clair. Fortunately, you can also do many things to improve your overall psychic and intuitive abilities.

In this chapter, we will explore the four clairs in more depth. Then, you'll find various tips and techniques for developing and refining your psychic abilities.

Intuition and Psychics

Did you know that to a certain degree, we are all psychic? We all have natural intuitive abilities. However, we tend to disregard them or underestimate them, particularly because we have very high expectations regarding what psychic abilities should be. We are all tricked into believing that psychic abilities are more complex and harder to achieve than they are. This is why most people think they are completely lofty and out of reach; therefore, they never attempt to strengthen them.

While not everyone wants to be psychic, a few realize that developing their intuitive abilities can serve them in numerous aspects of life. We experience the impact of intuition every day. Do you know why you feel oddly uncomfortable around a specific person? Or how you walk into a room and get an ill vibe? That is your intuition coming into play.

Our intuition is what safeguards us from potential harm or hurt. It instills our confidence in our knowledge, allowing us to make better and faster decisions. Our inner voice, or gut feeling, extends beyond normal logic and reason. It allows us to combine the information we have with who we essentially are so we can act accordingly. Intuition is also associated with heightened creativity, which fosters greater opportunities.

If you wish to pull cards, complete tarot readings, or are just interested in heightening your senses and easing your daily experiences, you should consider working on your intuitive abilities.

What Are the Clairs?

There are eight clair senses that we can tap into to receive unearthly information:

1. **Clairvoyance** - clear seeing
2. **Clairaudience** - clear hearing
3. **Claircognizance** - clear knowing
4. **Clairsentience** - clear feeling
5. **Clairgustance** - clear tasting
6. **Clairsalience** - clear smelling
7. **Clairempathy** - clear emotions
8. **Clairtangency** - clear touch

However, the first four clairs, which we will discuss in more depth, are the most important. They are indispensable when it comes to seeking guidance on our paths of growth and transformation. Focusing on these four can help us heighten our collective consciousness. Developing these clair abilities allows you to raise your empathy and intuition, which helps you nurture your relationships and improve your decision-making abilities.

Clairvoyance

When the word psychic comes up, most people immediately imagine a woman staring into a crystal ball, waiting for her client's future to unfold right before her eyes. This stereotype is perhaps the reason behind the term *clairvoyant*, which is believed to be synonymous with the word psychic. Many people don't realize that clairvoyance is just one of the numerous clairs and tools that a psychic uses.

A psychic receives clairvoyant messages or downloads as scenes, colors, dreams, visions, or imagery in their minds, or even externally, with their eyes. These messages aren't always straightforward and are often metaphorical. Yes, kind of like dreams!. For instance, an overwhelmed or stressed client may appear to be drowning. If someone is experiencing major life changes, the psychic may see the ground shaking beneath their feet. Fishing represents the search for new opportunities. Different readers may get different metaphors or downloads that differ from one client to the other.

Depending on how this ability manifests itself, different psychics use them for different purposes. Believe it or not, some people use their clairvoyant abilities to find lost items. It is not uncommon that you find a psychic with heightened visionary senses to help others find their keys, pets, etc. This gift does not only help their bearers grasp a deeper understanding of their souls and the souls of the entire universe, but they can also use it for the better good.

Clairaudience

Clairaudience refers to the ability to receive audible messages from a higher entity or the spiritual world. Those with clairaudient abilities can hear sounds that no one else can hear, surpassing the normal level of consciousness and the physical world. You must be incredibly intuitive to receive vocal messages from the spiritual realm.

The messages received may be very clear, meaning that the psychic may receive certain words or phrases or hear specific names, or they may be vague with music or other undiscernible sounds. The sounds often differ from what we usually hear in the physical world. Psychics may feel like the words are being spoken directly into their ears or inside their heads. They may also hear noises that echo from a different realm. They are usually tormenting and rather harsh. The sounds remain constant, with a calm, even tone. Some psychics hear the voices of their loved ones who have passed. Clairaudients usually receive their messages during significant times, such as emergencies or crises. The voices also make themselves heard to guide the psychic when they are at a crossroads for guidance. Some psychics hear the voices of spirits in their dreams. Most psychic downloads that are intended for clients are straightforward and short.

Many of those who have clairaudient abilities seldom realize it or speak of it. This is because hearing sounds that no one else can hear is a symptom of schizophrenia or psychosis. Even those who know all about clairaudience and are aware of their abilities may struggle to make sense of the messages they receive, especially when they are not straightforward or are just random sounds.

Clairsentience

Clairsentience messages are purely felt, making them the most common intuitive ability among these four clairs. Everyone has gut instincts, regardless of how strong or otherwise they are felt. Many people are also empathetic, which gives them the ability to sense other people's emotions or feel the overall vibe of a room. Clairsentient psychics can tell the energy of others as soon as they see them or start talking to them. While this is a significant intuitive ability, it can add a lot to reading when combined with other psychic abilities. Whenever a psychic receives a message, their clairsentience usually lets them know how important the information is for their client.

Those with high clairsentient abilities have access to the energies and feelings of people. They also sense the energies attached to certain objects, places, or events. They can easily relate to everything happening in front of them and the things that occur at different times and places. Their heightened intuition and empathy give them access to psychic-level information. This means they just "know" stuff with no logic or reason attached. Clairsentients know and feel things that have not been previously disclosed to them. While we can all get a feel for certain vibes or energies, clairsentients experience more intense feelings that can not be ignored. This intensity and pronounced clarity give them access to more information than the average empathetic person can obtain.

Clairsentients are easily drawn to strong vibrational energies, whether they are positive or negative. This is why they can tend to take things very personally and are likely to be burdened by the unhelpful emotions and experiences of others. This is also why they must always cleanse their energy fields and indulge in self-care practices.

If a clairsentient gives a person with physical ailments a reading, they will more than likely feel their client's condition in their own body. For instance, if someone is struggling with digestive issues, the psychic may feel tingling, or any other sensation, in their belly. If the client, or someone close to them, is experiencing knee joint pain, they will feel an ache in that area.

Claircognizance

Claircognizance is often confused with clairsentience because of how similar the abilities are. Like clairsentients, claircognizants just know things without proper logical reasoning. They just know the reality of things or can tell when things are about to happen, even though there are no signs indicating that. If you speak to a claircognizant psychic, they will be able to tell that you grew up with a narcissistic mother or just got out of a toxic relationship. Claircognizants can even tell that you struggle with your highly sensitive child because of how cautious you need to be around them. They do that by sharpening their intuition, surrounding subconscious obstructions, traumas, unhealed wounds, and past pains. They can tell exactly what is holding you back, and through that, they can reveal what kind of relationship patterns or complex connections you have in your life.

A claircognizant's intuition offers them an instant, large download of their client's struggles and life situation. Like clairsentient, they are encountered with a prominent gut feeling that they can not shake away, no matter how hard they try. The difference here is that the psychic download manifests as thoughts instead of sensing the energy or "feeling" the information.

For many claircognizants, their messages come through as light bulbs that light up inside the head. This phenomenon usually lasts for a flash of a second. Psychics can receive these intuitive news flashes at any time, whether working, watching television, working out, or painting. While you would expect them to be involved in an activity that is somewhat related to the information received, considering that they come in as thoughts, this is rarely the case.

Claircognizant abilities can be burdensome for many people, especially since they often warn them about the people they know and care about. After all, it is never good to learn that one of your closest friends has been lying to you. Nevertheless, even though there are some things that you think you are better off not knowing about, this ability can give you indispensable insights and knowledge. It can help guide you in numerous areas of your life.

Developing Psychic Abilities

It does not matter where you currently stand in your psychic journey or what your beliefs regarding psychics are because the chances are that you have your own intuitive psychic tendencies. Most spiritual and psychic individuals believe that we all have extraordinary inclinations. All we need to do is learn how to develop and refine them.

The words intuitive and psychic are almost synonymous. Being highly intuitive allows you to tap into your inner powers. When you achieve a high enough level of consciousness, you'll be able to feel, think, see, or hear things far beyond our physical world. Many people already unknowingly experience this phenomenon daily.

Intuition is perhaps the only gift that everyone in the world possesses. If you think about it, qualities and traits are only described as gifts when only a portion of the world has them, except for intuition. Everyone has it, but only a few people recognize its power and capitalize on it.

Refining Your Clairvoyance

1. Meditate

To develop your clairvoyant abilities, get in a comfortable position and breathe deeply and evenly. Make sure your breathing is rhythmic before shifting focus to your third eye chakra. Imagine that you are breathing light through this energy center throughout the entire meditation practice. Stay in this meditative state for as long as you desire and practice it regularly.

2. Gaze at the Sun

While this seems like a painful practice, it can significantly raise your vibrations and clear the clairvoyant communication pathways. Face the direction of the sun, directing your third eye toward it. Make sure to wear sunscreen and close your eyes! Moonlight gazing is also effective.

3. Activate Your Third Eye Chakra

Meditation, introspection, crystals such as amethyst, labradorite, sodalite, and yoga are just a few things that can help you activate your third eye chakra.

4. Improve Your Diet

Eat a balanced and healthy diet and focus on foods such as mushrooms, noni juice, and honey that help you support your third eye chakra.

5. Use Vibrations

Vibrate your third eye chakra by singing, chanting, humming, or using a singing bowl. This can help you clear any obstructions and stubborn energies, ensuring a free flow in your psychic communication channels.

6. Use Crystals and Essential Oils

Use selenite, clear quartz, lapis-lazuli, amethyst, or other third eye chakra crystals in your meditative practice. Place it on your forehead for the best results. You can also place the crystal on the mat as you practice yoga. Rubbing essential oils like rosemary, palo santo, frankincense, and lavender on your forehead is also highly effective.

Developing Clairaudience

1. Meditate

Get in a comfortable position before inhaling, filling your entire abdomen with air. Then, exhale forcefully. Do this a few times while keeping your consciousness within the physical frame of your being. Imagine that golden light is clearing the space around your ears and temples.

2. Clear Your Throat Chakra

Singing, chanting, and humming can help you clear your throat chakra. You should also avoid negative conversations and gossip.

3. Use Crystals

Hold healing stones like sodalite, selenite, and labradorite around your ears and temples. You can wear throat chakra crystals as earrings or necklaces if you wish. They can also be incorporated into your meditative and yoga practice.

4. Practice Active Listening

Sit down and breathe steadily and deeply. Keep your thoughts and emotions at bay as you focus on your surroundings. Listen to all the sounds around you, whether it is the wind, the running car engine in the street, the birds, or a panting dog.

Strengthening Your Clairsentience

1. Use Crystals

Hold crystals like rose quartz or unakite jasper close to your heart. As with other crystals, you can meditate with it or do yoga in its presence. You can also wear it as a pendant on a long necklace.

2. Create a Safe Space

Create a clutter-free space in your home that you can retreat to whenever you feel overwhelmed by external energies and emotions. You can also use this space to practice heart chakra-specific meditations and yoga poses.

3. Try Smudging

Use palo santo or sage to smudge your home and body to ground your aura.

Achieving Claircognizance

1. Practice Automatic Writing

You can either use an electronic device or pen and paper for this practice. Write down everything that comes to mind, regardless of how stupid it seems to be. Let your subconscious mind take the lead, allowing your consciousness to just watch.

2. Use Crystals

Using solar plexus chakra-specific crystals can help you clear your claircognizant communication pathways. These include citrine, tiger's eye, pyrite, amber, and golden apatite.

3. Meditation

Practicing any type of meditation for at least five minutes a day can help you heighten your intuitive senses. Over time, you'll be able to quiet your thoughts and tune into your intuition.

How often do you suddenly turn around because you can feel someone's eyes on you? Have you ever thought of someone just to find them ringing you up later in the day? Perhaps you have got the chills upon entering a room or had a bad feeling about a trip that ended up horrendous. These are not coincidences. They are your psychic gifts trying to tell you something. The first step toward developing your psychic abilities is learning to trust your intuition. It is there for a reason!

Chapter 7: Psychic Reiki Practicum 1 - Healing Yourself

Reiki energy can be a wonderful source of restorative power even Level one practitioners can apply. At this level, practitioners first learn how to heal themselves using their Reiki skills of energy manipulation and intuition. Later on, you'll also master how to use the same techniques to help others heal. This chapter is dedicated to teaching you self-healing methods to empower yourself when recuperating from a medical condition or injury. Helping others will be discussed in the following chapter. With its beginner-friendly exercises and comprehensive explanations, the techniques in this chapter will provide the perfect foundation for a new and healthier life.

Preparing Your Environment

Although Reiki is a universal life force within you, you must create an environment free of distractions and negative spiritual influences to enhance it with natural psychic energy. Make sure to find a place where you can stay safe, comfortable, and focused during your sessions. Unless you suffer from a medical condition that requires round-the-clock care, it is also recommended you perform the self-healing exercises alone. The beauty of Reiki's hand-healing techniques lies in their simplicity. Because they are so simple, they can be done in any position you feel comfortable with as long as you are in an environment where you can relax.

Try using it regularly once you find a space that fits all these requirements. It is fine to make changes when traveling, but try not to switch it around too much. In addition, if you feel more focused without any distracting noises, feel free to work in complete silence. That way, you can focus only on the sounds of your body and develop a deeper connection with your intuition. However, many practitioners prefer listening to relaxing music before and even during their Reiki sessions.

Activating Your Hands

Before you start practicing any Reiki healing technique, the first thing to learn is how to make your hand receptive to psychic energy. This involves sensing it with your hands and drawing it toward your palms. While Masters often ignore this step, beginner practitioners can not afford to do the same. Unlike them, you are just developing your connection with Reiki energy, and without the proper connection, you'll not have anything to use in the healing session.

The benefits of activating your hands include:

- Drawing more energy into your hands
- Symbol activation becomes easier
- You are showing respect to the energy, symbols, and your guides
- You are activating your chakras, the most energy-sensitive points of your body

There are several ways to activate your hands. Here is a simple way to do it:

- Sit or stand in a relaxed position and close your eyes.
- Take a deep breath, then exhale. Repeat until you feel your body and mind calming down.
- With your palms pointing forward, elevate your hands above your head. You can draw a symbol, hold a trinket in your hand or even call upon your spiritual guide during this process.
- Visualize the psychic energy above your head and see it entering through your crown chakra.
- Allow the energy to flow through your body until it reaches your hands.
- When you feel completely energized, you'll be ready to use Reiki.

Establishing a Deeper Connection

Having activated your hands, you'll feel confident and encouraged to do great things with your newfound power. However, you must remember that one or even a handful of successful connections does not guarantee that the Reiki energy will stay with you forever.

Here are a few tips to deepen this connection, so you can call on your intuitive power whenever you need it:

- Start your days with a quick session. 15-30 minutes of hands-on Reiki practice every morning after waking up will allow you to stay grounded through your day.
- Implement daily gratitude. Practice saying thanks for the energy and the help of symbols and spiritual guides aiding you during your session daily.
- Finish your day with Reiki. Repeat your morning technique before going to bed to have a restful sleep.
- Kill spare time with Reiki. Whether you are waiting in line in the grocery store, waiting for friends to arrive at a restaurant, or traveling on public transport, it is the ideal time for grounding Reiki exercises.
- Practice hand activation. Make the conscious decision to practice receiving Reiki energy through your palms as frequently as possible.
- Practice at your own pace. Feel free to take your time with the exercises, and do not worry about not practicing enough. Everyone has their own way of connecting to their intuition, so you know best what works for you.

Self-Healing Reiki Hand Movements

While it is good to have a dedicated time for your session, with an area established for practicing, you can do a session whenever you feel the need for it. You will simply go to this dedicated place, get comfortable, and relax with your preferred method. This can be music, breathing in silence, calling on spiritual guides, etc. Remove your shoes and go through the hand-activating or empowering step. If you lie down, place a pillow under your head and maybe a small blanket to cover your body. If not, just stay or sit in a comfortable position with your shoulders relaxed and slightly rolled back.

Close your eyes and proceed with scanning your body for areas that need healing. When you have identified the problematic areas, you can try to relax a little bit more by focusing on your breaths. This will also help you focus on performing the hand positions by employing all your energy. There are several different hand positions that you can apply during a self-healing process. Each of them is designed to assist in relieving the symptoms in a particular area of your body. While their description below should give you a great head start on how each of them should be performed, it is recommended that you focus on the areas where you have found issues while scanning.

Each hand movement should be applied for no more than 5 minutes at each session. It is better to repeat the exercises several times a day to ensure positive energy flow towards the desired areas than to swamp them with an overflow of energy all at once, as this can slow down the healing process. Below are the hand positions you can use for Reiki healing.

Face

Face position.
https://pxhere.com/en/photo/1616861

One of the first positions in Reiki's hand placement is the face position. It works for the issue associated with the throat and third eye chakras.

- Take a deep breath and raise your hands to your face
- Rest your palms against your face by covering your eyes and forehead

- Keep your hands there for the allocated time without applying any pressure

Crown

This position addresses issues in your crown chakra, alleviating headaches and other symptoms related to this region.

- Place your hands on either side of your head, palms resting above your ears and below the top of your head
- Take a deep breath and feel the energy coursing through your fingertips near your crown
- Keep breathing in and out and holding your head for four to five minutes or until you feel your symptoms dissipate

Back of the Head

As in the previous exercise, this hand position is also geared towards the head and spine-related symptoms and realigning the course of energy through your body.

- Close your eyes and cross your arms behind your head
- Put one hand just above the nape of your neck and the other one on the back of the head
- Inhale and let the energy flow through your body until you exhale
- Repeat for two to three minutes before opening your eyes

Jawline

This position aligns energy in your jawline and chin areas, alleviating symptoms in facial muscles, teeth, and gums.

- Cup your jawline with your hands, palms resting on your chin
- Secure your hold but do not put too much pressure on your jaw
- Inhale and exhale several times until you feel your jaw relaxing and the tension leaving this area

Chest

This is another great way to start your session, especially if you are working on several different areas and require the assistance of your spiritual guides.

Chest position.

- Join your hands in a prayer position in front of your chest. They should be joined just below your chin, a little higher than when reciting a prayer.

- Keep your hand joined while concentrating on your breathing for three to five minutes. Not exerting too much pressure with your hands will help you stay focused.

- Release the air from your lungs and lower your hands to your sides.

- Continue breathing in and out until you feel ready to either move on to the next hand placement or perform a post-treatment scan.

Shoulder Blades

The shoulders are crucial in supporting your body and the energetic flow through it. This hand placement will help restore this function.

- Put your hands flat on your shoulders, keeping your elbows bent. Then, raise your hands up over your head.
- If you can not reach it from behind, you can also place your hands on your shoulders from the front of your body. Your shoulders and hands should remain relaxed.
- Close your eyes and take deep breaths until you feel the tension dissipating

Neck, Collarbone, and Heart

The space between your neck and your heart is one of the most significant regions of your energetic systems, with numerous issues related to it.

- Form a V-shape with the thumb and the fingers of your non-dominant hand
- Place this hand on your neck, slightly cupping it
- Put your other hand between your heart and your collarbone
- Hold the position while breathing deeply for four to five minutes

Rib Cage

This hand placement heals the symptoms originating from your rib cage, which is essentially the pathway between your heart and solar plexus centers.

- Close your eyes and place one of your hands on the lower end of your breastbone
- Place the other hand slightly below the first one
- Inhale and relax your elbows to allow the energy to flow from your hands towards your rib cage
- Hold the position for two to three minutes

Abdominal Area

This hand placement is for healing digestion-related conditions and issues with endocrine glands located in your abdomen.

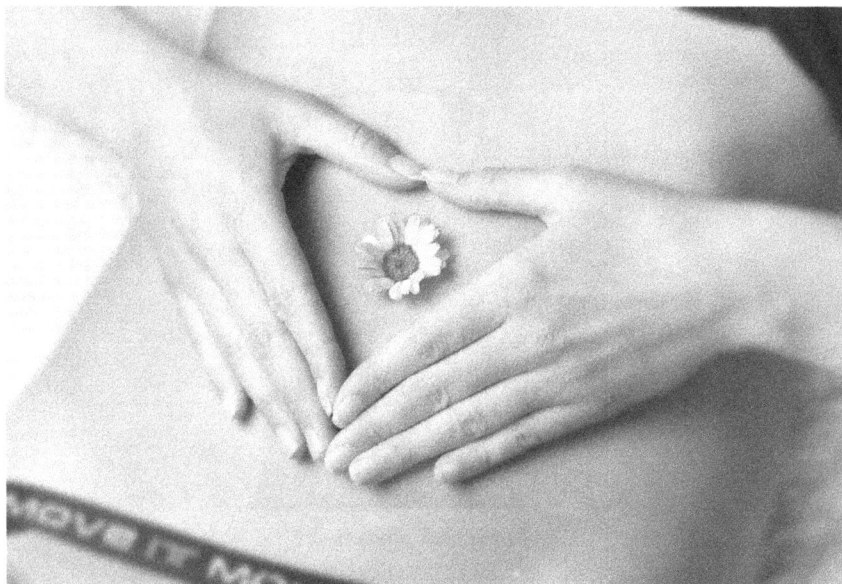

Abdominal position.

- Put your hands on your stomach, just above your navel
- Make sure your fingers are touching at the tips but not interlaced
- Relax your elbows and breath in and out for a few minutes

The Middle of Your Back

Placing your hands on the middle of your back supports your spine, reinforcing your resolution to combat your condition.

- With your elbows bent, move your hands behind your back
- Place your hands on your mid-back area and take a deep breath
- Hold the position for one or two minutes or until it feels comfortable to you

Lower Back

Hand placement on the lower back is beneficial for your entire energetic system as this area can be affected by myriad conditions.

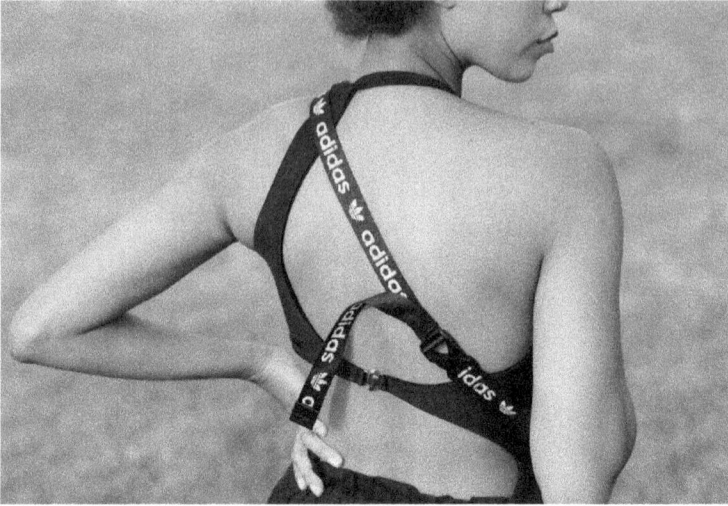

Lower back position.

- Start by reaching behind your back and putting your palms on your lower back. This is just below your rib cage, where your kidneys are.

- Make sure that your elbows are bent. If not, adjust the position until they are.

- Hold the position for the maximum allocated time, then release it with an exhale.

Pelvic Area

By placing your hands on your pelvic bones, you can ensure they provide sufficient protection for the organs they encapsulate.

- Place your hands on your pelvic bones, fingers pointing towards the middle of your pelvic region

- As with the rib cage placement, your fingertips should touch in the middle

- Breathe in and out for two to three minutes or until you feel your pelvic area relaxing

Sacrum

This hand placement is designed to relax the muscles in your sacral area and allow any illness related to this region to heal naturally.

- Take a deep breath and place your harm on your sacrum below your waist and kidneys

- Exhale and focus on sensing how your muscles and nerves relax in this area of your body
- Continue holding the pose for three to five minutes while breathing in and out deeply

Legs

If you have any root chakra or other grounding issues, this hand placement technique will help overcome them.

Leg position.
https://pixabay.com/es/photos/yoga-calma-liberar-extensi%c3%b3n-2662234/

- Start in a sitting position with your hands extended towards your legs
- Lean forward so that you can touch the soles of your feet. Do this one foot at a time
- If you can not reach the soles of your feet, you can place one of your hands on the top of your foot
- Crossing one leg over the other knee will help you reach both of your feet without having to twist your back to the side or strain your entire body unnecessarily
- Hold your hand on one of your feet for one to two minutes, then switch to the other one

Tips for Finding the Problematic Areas

As established early on in this book, Psychic Reiki is a highly intuitive practice. Not only do you need to use your instincts to sense the energy, but you must also channel it telepathically through your body. Any technique, including the hand positions presented in this practicum, is subject to individual interpretation. While they can be used as they are, their effects can be significantly heightened by putting your own interpretation on them.

You may wonder how you can intuitively scan your body and sense blockages. One of the most commonly used techniques for this purpose is called Byosen Reikan-ho. This self-scanning method, which involves feeling the resonance of a hand position, was taught by Usui himself. Before Byosen Reikan-ho is applied, you must activate your hands using your intuition, symbols, spiritual guides, and whatever aids you have chosen to employ. You may also want to clean the space and start scanning your body, starting from your head. Since the purpose of the scan is to reveal areas needing more attention, it is critical to be as receptive to the change in energy as you can during this process. The best way to find out if you are at the right place is to move your hand several times over the body part you sense the fluctuation taking place.

The latter can be used for any other technique you use for scanning, as well as Byosen Reikan-ho. Whichever scanning method you choose, make sure to repeat it before and after the healing session. This way, you can ensure that the treatment was completed successfully and evaluate whether it's working.

Disclaimer

It is important to note that Reiki energy should only be considered an empowerment tool for your healing journey and not an actual healing technique. If you suffer from any condition or injury, seek medical assistance for it first. After establishing the proper course of treatment with the help of a medical professional, you can consult them about alternative aids, such as Reiki. If they approve this method, you may use it to facilitate your healing experience and maintain your health after regaining it. Remember that while Reiki is a gentle healing technique, it is not appropriate for every illness. For example, Reiki energy can cause broken bones to heal very quickly. This could be a problem if the bones are not set properly. In this case, the doctor will not recommend Reiki until the bones are set and are at least partially healed. Reiki should not be used on active infections either, as it can heighten the discomfort.

Chapter 8: Psychic Reiki Practicum 2 - Healing Others

Once you have learned how to use Reiki healing techniques on yourself, you can move on to deepen your sense of intuition. This helps you to transfer your positive physic energy to others and support them in their healing journey. While you can start using hand placement techniques on others as a Level one practitioner, you'll learn more advanced techniques at Level two of your training. Apart from these advanced methods, the traditional Reiki symbols are also revealed in Level two, giving you a further tool for manipulating psychic energy. This chapter will explain several essential symbols and deal with practical advice for growing your intuition. We will also mention some advanced healing techniques that Reiki Masters have traditionally taught. Even if you are not ready to look into the advanced techniques, you can still combine the symbols with the blockage-sensing and simple hand placement methods mentioned in the previous chapter.

Improving Your Intuition

While intuition is something everyone is born with, as you have read in the previous chapter, there are plenty of ways to intensify it. Tapping into your intuitive powers is a prerequisite for healing yourself and others. If you want to move on from healing yourself to channeling your psychic energy to heal others, you must strengthen your intuition. Not only that, but sensing blockages in a body will require advanced, intuitive ability. You can use the Byosen Reikan-ho technique to improve your scanning abilities or look into other methods for the same purpose. You do not even have to use them as they are. As you do the entire scanning, sensing, and healing session, you can put a twist on any technique designed to build up your intuition. Remember, the power comes from within you, and the only way to get it out is by using the method that suits you.

You can practice enhancing your intuitive powers by yourself, or better yet, on another person. Of course, practicing with someone you know well is different from working with someone you can only get to know through intuition, but it will give you a head start, nevertheless. Ask them not to reveal anything about what they are feeling, then simply close your eyes and start focusing on your senses. Notice anything you feel, hear, or see; even close your eyes. The stimuli will unveil what your gut is telling you about the condition of the person in front of you. After repeating this several times, your ability to notice even the minor changes in someone's body will be heightened, and you'll be able to recall this power without even trying.

If you have trouble channeling your intuition to sense energy changes in others, you can ask your spiritual guides to help you out. You may not receive or have the ability to interpret the advice during the same practice session in which you made your request, but you'll certainly find it useful later on. Again, repetition is the key to successfully fine-tuning your intuitive abilities with the help of a higher spirit.

Sometimes you just have to look into what your gut is telling you and simply go with it. Ask a friend or family member to send you a photo of someone unknown to you. After contemplating every bit of information, you can intuitively gather about the unknown person and ask them to verify this information. Note everything you have gotten right, and try to call back the sensations you had when you received this information. You want to focus on these sensations next time you want to work on your intuitive powers.

Reiki Symbols

Reiki symbols are passed down by master's teaching Level two Reiki and onwards. Each sign works with specific characteristics that will help you channel psychic energy. However, the use of symbols is entirely up to the practitioner. Feel free to try them, but if you feel your intuition is enough to guide you through the healing session, you can omit using symbols. This may vary depending on your mental, physical, and spiritual state and the condition of your subject. Sometimes you'll not feel the need to reach for symbols at all. Whereas at other times, you'll be prompted to call on them for added reinforcement.

Types of Reiki Symbols

The main reason Reiki symbols are only revealed at Level two is that you must pass a certain spiritual threshold before you can call on them and harness their powers. And even then, it takes further spiritual growth before you can access all the symbols. Like crystals, symbols also differ in their vibration, which means that you'll need different symbols for awareness, healing, and achieving higher levels of consciousness.

Here is the list of benefits you can gain through different symbols:

- Balancing and aligning chakras and chakra systems
- Channeling Reiki into a problematic area
- Physical, mental, and spiritual healing,
- Clearing out blockages from chakras
- Attracting positive psychic energy
- Connecting with your spiritual guides
- Grounding yourself and others in the present
- Providing abundance in whatever you or others desire

Below are some Reiki symbols you can use in your practice. They can be applied as they are or modified to suit your purposes better. Not only that, but you can design your own symbols and use them. Nothing helps more with channeling intuitive power than the symbols created after an intrinsic vision.

Cho Ku Rei

Cho Ku Rei symbol.
Chokurei.jpg: Stephen Buck The Reiki Sanghaderivative work: LeonardoelRojo, CC BY-SA 2.0
<https://creativecommons.org/licenses/by-sa/2.0>, via Wikimedia Commons
https://commons.wikimedia.org/wiki/File:Chokurei.svg:

Also known as the Power symbol, Cho Ku Rei is a tool for changing the energy intensity in a particular chakra or body part. It allows you to transfer energy between your body and the body of the person you are healing. This symbol is represented as a coil, which you can use to increase or decrease power, depending on which direction you are drawing it. Cho Ku Rei is activated by visualizing a switch next to the symbol. Once activated, it will increase your ability to channel Reiki through your body and guide you through your session.

Sei He Ki

Sei He Ki symbol.
Stephen Buck The Reiki Sangha, CC BY-SA 4.0 <https://creativecommons.org/licenses/by-sa/4.0>, via Wikimedia Commons https://commons.wikimedia.org/wiki/File:Seiheiki.jpg:

Sei He Ki, or the Harmony symbol, is particularly good for mental clarity and emotional balance. Its name can be translated as "God and man become one," and it is often illustrated as either a bird's outstretched wings or a wave looming over a beach. This is a great symbol for promoting balance in the mind, bringing the two sides of a person together. It can also be used to ward off an imbalance.

Hon Sha Ze Sho Nen

Symbol of distance.
Stephen Buck The Reiki Sangha, CC BY-SA 4.0 <https://creativecommons.org/licenses/by-sa/4.0>, via Wikimedia Commons https://commons.wikimedia.org/wiki/File:Honshazeshonen.jpg:

The symbol of distance is often used for healing at a distance. It is a more complex symbol and is usually taught on higher levels. The direct translation talks about having no past, present, or future, speaking about reiki healing over long distances. For example, you can send Reiki through the symbol into someone's past and modify their experience by putting things into a different perspective. This will help them heal from past traumas and move on with their lives. You can also use the symbol to send energy into the future to prepare someone for a negative experience.

Shika Sei Ki Reiki

Shika Sei Ki Reiki's vibrations resonate with the heart chakra's energy and are used to treat any issues related to this center. It helps remove negative influences from the heart chakra, allowing the vital life force to flow through it once again. This eliminates negative emotions and thought patterns, revitalizing a person's mind, body, and soul.

Nin Giz Zida

This symbol is used for spiritual cleansing and is known as the serpent of fire. It channels energy through all the chakras, aligning them or balancing their functions. You can use it to relax your mind and body before a session or to bring the person you are working on into a state of serenity. Nin Giz Zida is often combined with other symbols for grounding, focusing intention, clearing energetic paths, and other purposes.

Shika So Reiki

Typically taught at Usui level two, Shika So Reiki is a symbol used to alleviate symptoms related to throat chakra blockages and malfunctions. This symbol can heal thyroid imbalances or other issues with boy regulation. On a wider scale, it can aid imbalances in a society or group.

The Dragon of Fire

The Dragon of Fire symbol can help form a connection with nature's psychic energy and balance the flow of different forms of power. Sometimes, a person's issues stem from a drastic difference in their vibrations and the vibrational energy of the universal life force around them. This symbol can help you realign the person's energy by challenging natural energy into them. It can also serve as a shield against negative energy when activated in front of the body.

How Reiki Symbols Work and How to Activate Them

Reiki symbols are carriers for the energy you harness from the spiritual world. Each sign is linked to several forms of energy and spiritual guides that emit healing vibrations. As a result, Reiki symbols can boost your psychic energy levels, healing your mind, body, and spirit during the process. When conducting energy through your body, you are doing this through intent. When you include symbols in your intention, your ability to channel the universal life force is magnified. They boost your vibration, allowing the energy to flow more freely and rapidly. This helps you uncover the root of chakra imbalances and blockages in your body and in the body of others, after which you can find the best way to heal them.

Before you can use any of the symbols, you must activate them with Reiki energy. There are a few ways to do this:

- **Drawing:** You can draw symbols on chakras, talismans, or wherever you may feel you can use them. If you are going to draw a symbol before a scan or treatment session, trace its outline with your index, thumb, index, and middle fingers joined together. This will concentrate the energy, making it easier to channel wherever you need it to travel.

- **Visualizing:** Symbols you use regularly will be engraved in your brain, which means you can simply envision using them. Just set your intention towards a symbol you know the benefits of, and it will soon be at your service.

- **Chanting Their Name:** If you have trouble visualizing a symbol, chant their name three times, and they will appear in the physical world.

Planting Symbols into a Person's Energy Field

This is one of the most common ways to use symbols in your practice. It is very subtle yet powerful, making it perfect for beginners needing a major boost when learning their trade. You may initially struggle with emotional blocks or unwanted thoughts during your healing sessions. Even if you learn how to dismiss these from your own thoughts, you may find them way harder to deal with in someone else's body and mind. By placing empowering symbols into their energy field, you can keep the distracting thought patterns at bay even after the session.

The planting technique is particularly beneficial in cases when you can not apply hand placement techniques due to specific injuries or conditions. It is easier to use than distance healing but will have the same powerful effect. Typically, it is applied through the crown chakra as this is the best way to channel Reiki through someone. This works on the same principle as when you are receiving empowering energy when you are preparing yourself for healing.

Traditional Reiki Techniques

As mentioned earlier, traditional Reiki approaches are only taught by masters on all levels. Here are a few examples of the techniques you can learn as a Reiki practitioner:

- **Gassho Meiso:** A meditation technique to help you focus your mind and energy during a healing session
- **Joshin Kokyu-Ho:** Breathing exercise that strengthens and cleanses your spirit
- **Kenyoku:** Also called dry bathing, it helps you leave all distractions behind and ground you to the present
- **Reiki Mawashi:** A group exercise that allows several practitioners to share their psychic energy, empowering each other in the process
- **Nats -Ho:** Another detoxification technique for your mind, body, and soul
- **Enkaku Chiryo:** Also known as Shashin Chiryo, a distance healing technique that teaches how to make associations through photographs, names, etc.
- **Gyoshi-Ho and Koki-Ho:** The first one teaches healing with eyes, the second with the breath (they are always taught together)
- **Seiheki Chiryo:** This allows you to heal unhealthy habits and addictive behavior by transforming them into healthy ones
- **Nentatsu-Ho:** Used to deprogram someone's mind to remove unwanted through processes
- **Jacki-Kiri Joka-Ho:** This technique teaches how to transform negative energy present in an object into positive energy you can use for reinforcement

- **Byogen Chiryo:** Helps reveal and treat the origin of certain conditions, mainly mental ones
- **Tanden Chiryo:** A psychic power-up tool for yourself or the person you want to heal

If you have trouble determining which technique to use on others, you can use the ***Reiji-ho technique*** to guide you. Its name is translated as the indication of the spirit, which means you'll receive assistance from the Spirit of Reiki. Essentially, this is another way to enhance your intuition when scanning someone's energy field for possible issues. Apart from the technique itself, Reiji-ho can also reveal the symbols and hand placements you should use during your session. Depending on the malady you are dealing with and your experience level, you may also need to use Reiji-ho during the session. Feel free to use it anytime you need guidance, even if you have already used certain treatments for specific conditions. Remember, each person has a unique constitution and energetic field. A treatment that works for one person may not work for another person with the same condition. This is exactly why you need to rely on your intuition.

Disclaimer

Once again, you are reminded that while Psychic Reiki is a valuable power enhancement tool, it is not an officially recognized healing technique. This is even more critical to emphasize when you have others that rely on your help on their healing journey. Advise them that if they suffer from any condition or injury, they should seek medical assistance for it first. After establishing the proper course of treatment with the help of a medical professional and getting their approval for alternative aids, such as Reiki, your client can turn to you for Reiki healing sessions. Certain conditions cannot be treated with psychic healing, regardless of how mild the method you are using. Other times, the medical professional will advise against certain techniques such as direct hand placement but approve distance healing, or vice versa.

People with an active infection or undergoing cancer treatment should not be treated with Reiki. Firstly, while the healing energy can remove the toxins, it could help spread them, aggravating the condition. Secondly, the toxins are part of the treatment and should not be removed from the body. As the frequency of energetic vibrations may trigger seizures or disrupt the work of pacemakers, people who have epilepsy or who have pacemakers should not be treated with Reiki healing.

Chapter 9: Psychic Reiki Practicum 3 - Psychic Distance Healing

All the intuition-boosting techniques you were introduced to in the previous two chapters can be a stepping stone to more advanced healing techniques for yourself and others. They can also become a tool to prepare your body and mind to hone your telepathic abilities and venture into distance healing. This chapter discusses this unique form of healing, which allows you to alleviate symptoms without being in the same room as the person you are treating. You will learn how this technique works in the traditional system and how you can use your psychic powers to personalize the method. This will allow you to find the therapy suitable for you and the person you are treating, and you'll be more effective.

How Distance Healing Works

After learning about the benefits of hand placement techniques and healing through energy transfer in one-on-one and group sessions, you may wonder how Reiki works at a distance. Is energy not weakened when sent through a greater distance? And if it is, what is the purpose of sending it to someone who needs empowerment? The answer to these questions is not that clear-cut. Traditional energetic waves are prone to fatigue when crossing great distances, but the ones you create in your brain when using your psychic abilities are not. This is why you can send Reiki telepathically across space and time. If someone across the world needs a boost of energy to deal with physical and mental conditions, you can send it to them through distance healing techniques.

Healing from the Past

While you cannot change anyone's past, you can put their experiences into a different perspective through Reiki healing. Traumatic experiences from the past often lead to chakra imbalances in the present. In fact, it is more common for people with emotional trauma to seek Reiki treatment than people suffering from other conditions. When someone's past affects their present life, it can be easily picked up during the initial session, even if they do not talk about it beforehand. People often can not help but think about the trauma during the session, even when asked to relax. You will definitely sense this when you connect to them telepathically. Fortunately, you can bring painful memories to the surface and envelop them in positive energy. This changes the patterns around them, so the recipient can move on with their life.

Healing in the Present

Healing in the present time is particularly useful for critical situations, such as when someone needs your help immediately, and they cannot get to you. In this case, you can send a high amount of positive energy as soon as you are notified of the situation. However, things do not need to be urgent to send Reiki in the present, and it is sometimes simply more convenient to do it this way.

Healing in the Future

While it is far less common, distance healing is also used to send Reiki into the future. If someone has an upcoming event, appointment, or interview they feel anxious about, energy sent ahead of time can calm their nerves and help them get through the situation confidently. Even knowing they will be able to rely on this little boost when the time comes can reduce their stress and keep their health and happiness balanced.

Preparatory Steps for Distance Healing

Depending on individual circumstances, distance healing can be initiated in several different ways. Regardless of the method you choose, there are several steps you should follow. First and foremost, you should always inform the person about your intent and get their consent before actually sending the restorative energy life force. Make sure to share as many details about the transfer as possible so they can prepare themselves to receive the power boost. This should include the exact date and time you'll send the energy and instructions on what they should or should not do during the transfer.

When you tell a person about your intent, encourage them to discuss what they hope to achieve with the treatment. Ask them about the state of their health and whether their doctor approves of Reiki as an alternative treatment if they have a health condition. Once everything is clear on both sides, you can remind them when you'll be sending energy. You may also call or message them before you start channeling Reiki. This is an optional step to ensure they are in a stress-free environment where they will not be distracted by anything or anyone.

Essentially, all your client needs to do when receiving Reiki from a distance is to sit down or lie back and relax. Ideally, they should be in their homes to receive it, but they can choose to do it at their workplace during lunch. As long as they stay still during the transfer, they can pick the best time and place that suits them. The transfer can last from 10 minutes to an hour, depending on how much boost they need.

Using the Reiki Distance-Healing Symbol

When it comes to sending Reiki, every Reiki Practitioner has their own preferences. Their approach often depends on what the recipient wants to achieve. The most commonly used method uses the distant healing symbol, Hon-Sha-Ze-Sho-Nen, combined with one or more other empowering symbols like Cho Ku Rei and Sei-He Ki.

Cho Ku Rei, the power symbol, is often used in distance healing in a traditional sequence called the Reiki Sandwich. While the sequence can be used for other purposes, in this case, it consists of two power symbols and the distance healing symbol in the middle. Here is how to do this method:

- Write the recipient's name and the purpose of the treatment on a piece of paper. Fold it and keep it in your hands, palms facing each other.
- Let your body relax and allow your eyes to close.
- Repeat what's written on the paper, visualize Cho Ku Rei, and connect to the energy of the symbol.
- Now switch your intent towards Hon-Sha-Ze-Sho-Nen and visualize it beside or on top of Cho Ku Rei.
- Follow up with another Cho Ku Rei, which you can place on top or on the other side of Hon-Sha-Ze-Sho-Nen.

- Now, Hon-Sha-Ze-Sho-Nen is empowered on both sides, and you'll be able to see where to use it in your client's chakra system.
- You can start transferring the sequence into the recipient's mind along with the boost of a positive life force.
- When sending Reiki, do not try to channel it towards a specific area. The highest interest of the receiver is to get empowered mentally, so they can deal with their issues, whether physical or mental.
- Visualize the energy enveloping your client and soak in every detail of your experience as you may want to share it with them in the future.

When the transfer has been completed, let the client digest the new sensation for a few minutes or hours. Later on, you can ask them about their experience. If they describe feeling more relaxed than before, the new vital force is now taking effect in their body. Depending on their goals, some clients may experience an emotional release or have visions of certain activities, objects, or events.

If they had a visual experience, you could compare it to yours and see if there were any similarities between what you both saw. This will help you develop your telepathic abilities even more. Not only that, but if clients need any additional help, you'll be able to connect to them even faster.

Other Ways to Channel Energy

Apart from the traditional distance healing technique, there are several other ways to connect with the person you are trying to heal. Ideally, the connection should be made telepathically as this is the best way to transfer energy. However, using the tips at the beginning of this book, you can also use visualization techniques or any other psychic abilities that you have developed. Visualization techniques used for this purpose involve inspecting the person's chakra system and finding blockages, conjuring an image of their aura, and much more. Here are some methods you can try:

Use a Photo

Ask your client to send you a photo of themselves, preferably a full body shot. This can serve you as a visual aid for your intuition. Look at the image and contours of their body and try to imagine their aura as a bright light enveloping them. Search for any dark spots which will be where energy is needed most. You can do the same with their chakras, except you need to look a little harder for specific clues that indicate an imbalance. Once you have established the source of the problem, you can use telepathy to send Reiki right to the body part where it is most needed. At the end of the session, visualize how the transferred energy envelops the problematic area.

Use a Surrogate

If you do not have a recipient's picture, you can also use a surrogate object to make a connection. This can be anything from a personal belonging, a doll that looks like them, to a random item that you can associate with the person. Set your intention while holding this object and visualize your energy enveloping it. You can combine this with the sandwich sequence or simply hold the distance healing symbol over the surrogate body just as you do with the name on the paper method. Using your psychic powers, try sensing where the energy is needed. See how the energy is transferred to the surrogate and on to the recipient. An added benefit of this method is that you can see which areas of their body need more attention. After a check-in with your intuition, you'll know where the root of the issue is. You can even visualize the object representing that particular part of the body and not necessarily the entire body. While you can not send physical energy directly to the affected area, you can make this an intent through the telepathic transfer. The recipient's mind will register it as their own intent and focus its energy on repairing the issue.

Using Other Symbols

Should you choose not to use the traditional Reiki Sandwich sequence, you can even leave out using symbols. You can choose to empower yourself with only one if you feel you only need a little assistance. You can also draw your own symbols, which can have multiple benefits. This helps sharpen your intuitive powers like any other technique involving listening to your gut does. Instead of drawing or visualizing a traditional symbol after focusing on your intent, you just draw or imagine whatever sign comes to mind first.

In fact, you can even do this without concentrating on the treatment you are trying to provide. Your mind is the most relaxed when it does not have to deal with the pressure of performing, and this is exactly the right time to tap into your intuition. Do something that relaxes you, and keep a pen and paper beside you. This way, you can free draw a symbol whenever it comes to you.

The other huge benefit of drawing individual symbols for treating others is that they allow you to create deeper connections. After scanning a person's body in real life, you become aware of any potential issues in their chakra system. This is not the case with distance healing, so connecting with a person's energy system and channeling your power into it is inherently more challenging. However, by getting to know them and using your intuition, you can find the right symbol to boost your ability to channel the vital life force through time and space. A symbol designed for a person's specific needs will always allow you to make stronger telepathic connections.

A person needing a vital life force is not the only entity you can form powerful telepathic connections using your intuition. If needed, you can also use your psychic abilities to request assistance from your spiritual guides or the Spirit of Reiki. Just as they can help you find the right course of treatment, so can they send a symbol to enhance your abilities.

Benefits of Distance Healing

Besides the obvious factor of enabling you to help anywhere, anytime, distance healing comes with plenty of other benefits for you and your client. When channeling energy with your psychic abilities, you raise positive vibrations that keep the negative ones at bay. The more powerful the energy bursts are, as they have to be for you to send them through space and time, and the more often they happen, the cleaner your environment will be.

Distance healing eliminates the need to cleanse your space before each client. Since you do not have to prepare your workspace for each client, you can have a larger client base. Consequently, you can help more people who need this precious life force. Many people don't have Reiki practitioners available in their area, and traveling to one would increase their discomfort. Through distance healing, everyone can get the relief they need.

Some people may not feel comfortable enough in your workspace to just sit or lay down, close their eyes, and relax their body and mind. However, if they can do this in the comfort of their homes, they will become much more relaxed and ready to embrace Reiki in no time.

At the end of the day, distance healing is a much safer and more effective method of distributing Reiki energy. With powerful positive emotions, you can send an enormous boost to someone's chakra system in just a few minutes. If someone needs quick assistance in an unexpected situation, you'll be able to help them out regardless of your location.

Disclaimer

Since distance can affect the efficiency of the treatment, there are fewer contraindications than for hand placement or any other treatment conducted close to your subject. And as vibrations are being transformed over an extended period, they will not have such a drastic effect on the person's body. Instead, the gradual changes have long-lasting benefits improving their lives and making them happier and healthier. That said, distance healing is still a much-debated alternative healing method, which is not recognized by medical professionals either. The same rules apply to other Reiki sessions. Any medical condition should be treated with conventional medicine, and the physical energy should only serve as an aid.

This assistance should not be provided during surgery, particularly if the person is undergoing general anesthesia. Being under anesthesia prevents the mind from regulating its functions. Any alterations to one's energy system during this period can cause issues during and after surgery. You need to be aware of this as you are honing your telepathic abilities. For example, if someone close to you is having surgery, you may intuitively want to send them Reiki energy to help them get through the procedure. Make sure to wait until they start their post-operative recovery process to send them healing energy.

Chapter 10: Activate Your Third Eye Temple

The journey to one's Third Eye Temple involves different techniques. The landscape within the Third Eye chakra can be used for various psychic purposes and is ideal for enhancing psychic healing. This chapter explains the measures you can take to activate your third eye temple. We also cover the following aspects:

- What you can do in this temple
- How can the temple be used?
- What can you ask your guides?
- How do you solve specific problems or heal blockages?

We will give you insight into the different purposes for which you can use your Third Eye area in Reiki and explain through detailed steps how to connect with Reiki through the Third Eye.

Understanding the Third Eye Temple

Also known as the sixth chakra or sixth sense in the body, and situated in the center of your forehead, parallel to your eyebrows, it is believed to be connected to awareness, perception, and spiritual communication.

When this chakra is utilized, great insight and wisdom can be found. It also deepens your spiritual connection, which is extremely useful for healing.

The third eye chakra relates to traits like concentration, clarity, intuition, imagination, universal connection, and spiritual perception. It is believed to be connected to the cone-shaped, pea-sized pineal gland. It is viewed as a critical tool by mystics and seers and is believed to provide a universal connection. Most cultures recognize the pineal gland as being biologically linked to the third eye chakra.

What Can the Third Eye Chakra Do?

The chakra is viewed as the gateway to the spiritual world, including all psychic things. It also helps you get clear vision, removes mental blockages, and improves your mental flexibility. Many cultures see it as the most important sense – *and activating it is critical.*

If your third eye chakra is blocked, you'll probably feel fatigued, stuck, have low creativity, be pessimistic, fear success, lack motivation, and will repress memories. You may also face different problems – including confusion and uncertainty. The third eye sees the true world and its spiritual connections, whereas our eyes see the physical aspects. If you experience any of these signs, it means that your third eye must be activated. There are many advantages to activating your Third eye temple. When your third eye is opened, your mind becomes calmer and more focused. Whatever you do in life for a living, you are likely to experience a positive change following the activation of the third eye. The following are some of the experiences that come with opening your third eye chakra.

- **Wisdom:** Third eye activation gives you wisdom, enlightening you so that you can separate the truth from illusion. In other words, it gives you the wisdom of enlightenment.

- **Better Attention:** Your attention to detail significantly improves if your third eye is open. Your mind becomes more focused, and you'll have a heightened awareness of things that happen around you. Your senses of hearing, sight, and taste become sharper.

- **Enjoy Peace:** When your third eye chakra is activated, you can enjoy more peace, and anger issues will subside. You will find that irritation and anger will no longer affect you when the eye is open, and you'll feel at peace. Third eye activation also leads to a deep sense of calmness in your mind.

- **Devotion:** Third eye activation leads to devotion, which is an experience of the heart. Mental clarity leads to focus and improved concentration. It gives you insight and decisiveness when dealing with different issues.

How the Third Eye Affects Our Mental Health

The third eye chakra can affect us emotionally and spiritually in many ways, although mainstream science does not support the link. Yet, there have been many anecdotal reports of unexplained happenings connected to the third eye. It can often be used as a gateway to the spirit world. The following are some of the effects of telepathy on our minds.

Telepathy

Telepathy involves direct communication between two minds and is not just a myth. The mind can perceive someone else's thoughts without using recognized senses. This is known as telepathic communication, where the mind transmits information to another mind. When another person's beliefs or thoughts influence someone's mind, it is known as mind control.

Mind control can be influenced by the third eye temple, where influence comes from outside. However, it can also lead to destruction, and this is usually determined by the person imposing their power on someone's mind. The kind of knowledge passed through telepathic communication offers benefits and disadvantages, so you must believe your instincts.

Clairvoyance

Clairvoyance helps you predict the future, which can be influenced by your third eye when activated. The energy center also helps you do more than predict the future. You will be aware of the big picture when you open your third eye. The ability to see everything helps shift your perspective, so you can have a clear view of your blind spots and understand everything from the collective perspective. However, to use your third eye to see through space and time, you must first use it to see yourself.

Lucid Dreaming

Lucid dreaming happens when you are conscious, and many people have experienced this in their lifetime. It is a form of meta-cognition or awareness of your consciousness. During a lucid dream, you control what happens, which is only possible if your third eye chakra is open. In some cases, dreams come true, and they can give you guidance in your life. If you activate your third eye, you can interpret dreams.

How to Open Your Third Eye

The rituals to open your third eye should not be complicated since they include simple steps. The following are some methods you can consider opening the third eye.

Touch

You can use touch to awaken the energy in your third eye temple. You can use your finger to press or tap the third eye, and you need to recite your favorite affirmation while touching the temple. This is a simple ritual you can do anywhere, and it does not require special tools or equipment to perform.

Visualization

Visualization is another technique that you can consider for awakening your third eye. This process requires focus, so anything that can improve your attention will help open it. The method of visualization involves the following three steps.

- Hold any object in front of your eyes and try to study its details. Take your time to record your observations in your mind.

- Close your eyes and try to visualize the object you have been holding. Take about 30 minutes trying to concentrate on the item you studied.

- Repeat the process every day. You can also extend your concentration time and practice with more complex objects.

This exercise helps ground your vision so you can handle the insights that require higher consciousness.

Activate the Third Eye Chakra

To activate your third eye, begin by sending gratitude to it. This will stimulate your intuitive abilities and connection to nature. Your pineal gland regulates your sleep-wake cycle, which is important for properly opening your third eye.

Supplement Your Diet

If you eat well, you can do much more, including opening your third eye. There are many foods you can include in your diet that will support your third eye – and some that will limit you. Eat lots of nuts, berries, garlic, seeds, coconut, honey, herbs, and foods with vitamin D3. These all help with your pineal gland, which, in turn, supports the third eye.

Apply Essential Oils

Essential oils can heal ailments.
https://pixabay.com/images/id-3532970/

Essential oils can heal many ailments and boost your health – and they can also work wonders for opening your third eye. You can create your own essential oil blends, and most essential oils will be beneficial, but jasmine and sandalwood are recommended. Always use a carrier oil to dilute the essential oils to make sure the blend is safe.

When mixing in a carrier oil, you don't need much essential oil, and 5-7 drops will suffice. Because your third eye is between the eyes, dab a little on your forehead to open your third eye. Remember to use your chant as you apply the oil and once it is applied.

Sun Gazing

You can harness the power of the sun to awaken your third eye. Never look directly at the sun when it is in the sky, but gaze close to it at sunrise and sunset. Spend a few minutes each time, and you can also meditate as you do this to better awaken the third eye. The sun's power affects your pineal gland, activating the third eye.

Meditate and Chant

Meditation plays a pivotal role in activating the pineal gland through intention and vibration. It helps channel our energies, improve concentration, and remove negative toxins from the body. The third eye connects us to our gut feelings and works ahead of our five senses. However, to enjoy the benefits of the sixth sense, you must open your dormant eye. This is where meditation comes in handy and is viewed as the best way to awaken and activate your third eye.

There are different forms of meditation you can consider, and these are designed to help you improve your awareness and shift your consciousness to a higher level. This will help you remove anxiety and other forms of worry. Meditation also helps your mind work to the fullest and improves concentration.

Like any form of meditation, you must stay calm in a quiet environment and listen to the soothing sounds of music. Try to find a perfect place to sit comfortably on the chair or floor. You should relax your shoulders, keep your spine erect, and your hands on your knees. Other parts of your body like the stomach, face, and jaw must be relaxed, and make sure that your body is open to positive energy.

You can begin by bringing your index finger to the thumb and gently closing your eyes. Breathe slowly, and make sure you use your nose to inhale and exhale with your eyes still closed. Try to look at the third eye between your eyebrows; you can also use your fingers to locate it. While breathing slowly, try to channel your gaze at this point and concentrate on it for some minutes. Continue doing this until you see bluish-white or white light beginning to appear. When you reach this stage, you enter a stage of healing, and your concentration will be at the highest level and most effective. You want to let go of bad energies at this stage, and focus should be your top priority.

Chant as you meditate to help the bone in your nose to resonate. This will stimulate the pineal gland that is linked to your third eye. Chanting also helps you to focus on the things you are grateful for in your life. When you meditate, it is vital to appreciate the significance of the third eye. What you chant should come from your heart, and make sure that you include the things you want to achieve once your third eye chakra is activated.

Meditation is a simple exercise since there is no strict rule to follow. Stay in your meditation position for a few seconds, then blink your eyes. You can continue with your regular activities when you are finished. You can meditate every morning or a few minutes before going to bed. This will work wonders in healing and activating your chakras. Just make sure that you are focused on what you want to achieve regarding your third eye chakra.

Use Crystals

Crystals have healing energies and are believed to be crucial in opening your third eye. Choose purple colors of gemstones to boost your third eye.

Purple, and similar colors, are excellent for creating balance, opening the third eye, and signing the self.

Place the crystals of gemstones between your eyes on top of your third eye. Gemstones are believed to possess the energy that can stimulate your chakras. Different stones are used for various purposes, so you must choose the ones that suit your needs.

How Long Does Your Third Eye Chakra Take to Open?

That depends on the person. It will change from person to person and will also change during the year and even by the time of day. And, even if you do open your third eye, it is considered a lifelong practice that you never truly master—only improve on. You can dedicate as much time as you like each day to opening your third eye, and fifteen minutes every day should be sufficient using the above practices. Don't force it; wait for the eye to open naturally - as if you are waking from sleep.

How Do You Know If Your Third Eye Is Open?

Your third eye chakra is your sixth sense, and that is going to help guide you intuitively through life, so if you feel your sixth sense is helping you, then your chakra is likely to open. Use your intuition to develop your third eye once it is open. Your sixth sense is also linked to wisdom, growth, healing, and the spirit. Meditate even if you think your eye is open, and continue to practice each day while maintaining your health.

Chapter 11: The Psychic Reiki Toolkit: Crystals, Talismans, Trinkets, and Tarot

Everything in life is connected by energy, and Reiki healing makes the most of this energy field. This chapter will discuss the tools you'll need in your healing kit, from crystal to tarot and everything in between. And we discuss how you can use each one and the expected outcome they can bring to your healing practice.

Crystals and Gemstones

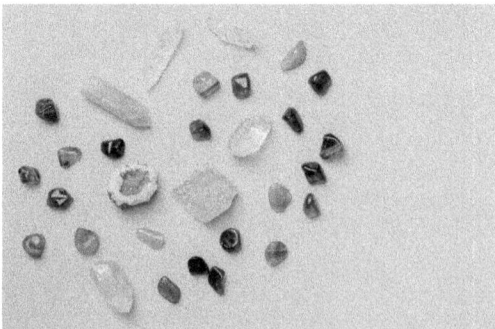

Crystals are conduits for the earth's healing energy.

When used properly, crystals are conduits for the earth's healing energy. They emit uplifting, positive, calming, and energizing vibrations that help your mind to be revitalized and peaceful. There are different types of crystals or gemstones, and each piece has a specific use on the body and mind. The vibrations and energies produced by crystals have healing powers, and they affect us in various ways. However, medical experts say no scientific research supports the efficacy of crystals in healing diseases.

Although there are mixed reactions to the healing powers of crystals, these stones have some form of physical and mental benefits, which can be attributed to the placebo effect. Many people have great faith in the healing power of prayer, and the same applies to crystals. The placebo effect is supported by scientific research, and the other thing is that crystals do not cause any harm to your health. Adding gems to your life can increase your confidence and positive energy.

When choosing gemstones, you must determine your wellness needs because different crystals are used for different ailments. These precious stones come in different colors and can be used as jewelry. Some give you a sense of calm when you carry them with you, and different crystals are good for helping you to meditate. The following are the types of crystals you can include in your toolkit.

- Clear quartz is ideal for beginners since it provides more energy and also charges your intentions when meditating.
- Black Tourmaline has protective properties and will guard you against negative energy. To protect your environment, place this stone on your desk, at your front door, or in the corners of your room to secure the environment.
- Amethysts offer calming energy and help you relax at night. You can put this stone under your pillow for a peaceful sleep. This crystal is good for you, particularly after a hectic day.
- Citrine represents light, joy, and happiness. If you are feeling low, you can invoke the powers of this stone.
- Aquamarine can be worn as a necklace and helps you speak the truth. This type of stone is a good accessory if you have speech deficiency. The stone also helps you achieve your goals when undertaking creative projects.
- Rose Quartz is associated with love and helps open your heart. You can keep it in your bedroom for consistent results.
- Tiger's Eye is a grounding stone that helps improve your physical performance in different activities like sports.

- Moonstone helps your heart when you are feeling low.
- Pink opal helps you release anger and tension.
- Kyanite is good for daily life and bolsters the mind and body link.

Regardless of what crystal you choose, make sure that you charge it by leaving it to sit outside in direct moonlight or sunlight for about four hours. Sunlight and moonlight are crucial as they help your crystal hold more energy. A charged crystal can support you in a way you may not see, but you'll feel the impact.

You must set clear intentions and visualize how you'll achieve your goals. You can achieve this by holding the stones in your hands and sitting quietly. Start thinking about your goals; the stone will absorb your intention and activate. Once it is charged, you can use it any way you like. For instance, you can wear it as a necklace, keep it in your office, or simply hold it whenever you want to revive your intention. Healing stones can be used together with other practices such as meditation.

Scrying Spheres and Bowls

The process of gazing into a bowl or crystal ball is known as scrying, and it is mainly used to divine the unknown. The goal of scrying is to help you receive or see messages, pictures, scenes, or symbols that possess information not previously known. There are different types of tools that can be used, like scrying spheres, bowls, or crystal balls. You can also consider cloud and water scrying.

When you look into the surface of your chosen item, your third eye will begin to separate from your body, and you'll feel as if you are meditating. You will see darkness in your vision; half of it should be black. When you reach this state, you'll begin to hear voices or see messages, pictures, and symbols. If you want to scry in a bowl or crystal ball, you need to follow the steps below.

- Take out the ball from its storage to set up the stage.
- Cleanse the ball using your favorite, most effective way.
- Create a sacred space where you can put your crystal ball at a comfortable height so you can easily gaze into it. Light a few candles, use sage to cleanse the space, light your favorite incense and turn on your favorite music.

- Turn on a voice recording app, so you do not miss crucial details that you might miss if you are just trying to write everything down.

- Sit comfortably as this process can take a long time.

- Begin gazing and count backward from 12, and try to visualize each number in the ball.

- When you are done with your countdown, take some time to look into the center of the ball, and you'll begin to see dark spots, black blobs, or clouds. This marks the beginning of your vision, and you must ensure that you lock your vision on the dark clouds once you see them.

- Ask questions when you begin to hear something from the clouds. Say everything you hear aloud so you can record it.

- End your session by counting from 1 to 12, and thank the spirits for guiding you.

- Cleanse the tools and put them back in their storage.

You should practice scrying often because it helps you fall into a trance quickly. Remember to choose an appropriate tool for your session. You can practice this healing method whenever you need answers to something you feel is impacting your life.

Tarot/Oracle Cards

Tarot and oracle cards can also be used for different purposes in Reiki. The readings are mainly used for clairvoyant sessions where the reader interprets messages conveyed by the tarot cards. You can ask anything you want; the readings are usually conducted in about 30 minutes. The cards will focus on all the different things you want to know.

If you want to know something about your career, you can ask the tarot cards, and you'll get your answer from an interpreter. You can also learn to interpret the messages, but this can take time. In any session, you can use direct questioning, and the reader will be able to give you answers related to your finances, work, and other areas that can affect your life.

Talismans and Sacred Items

Talismans and other sacred items are symbols of protection and can be used in various situations. For instance, you can use a protective talisman to protect your space, as well as protect memories from unwanted disruption or negative energy. Talismans can be worn, or you can keep them in appropriate places where they can protect.

The Reiki source energy can also be infused into crystals, which magnifies their healing power. A talisman or bracelet consists of various healing crystals that magnify the purpose of intent when infused. One thing about crystals is that they consist of different charms and energy that can solve various issues in life.

Reiki-infused jewelry is also used to provide support or boost your intentions. You can also get a talisman when you need a dose of love. If you are busy with other commitments, an amulet will provide quick healing or a solution to your problem. You can wear your charged bracelet the way you want, providing healing powers. Others wear bracelets to keep evil spirits at bay.

Trinkets

Like talismans, different types of trinkets can be used in Reiki sessions. Common trinkets include jewelry, heirlooms, figurines, and anything meaningful to the practitioner. These items can also be used to send telepathic healing messages. Your trinket can give you the power to communicate with other people or simply receive messages.

You can also get a bracelet that holds healing powers or is capable of keeping you calm. These bracelets are made from different materials and come in different shapes and sizes. Before you buy a bracelet, you should spell your intention and outline the goals you want to achieve. Understanding the purpose of each material used in the bracelet is vital. You can also use the Reiki charged bracelet in healing sessions and must state your intention.

Reiki Water

Wondering how you can charge water with Reiki? You can use your charged water for drinking, watering plants, or for any other healing work. Making Reiki water is simple as the entire process only requires your intention. Churches use prayers to charge their water while blessings of the spirit are invoked in sacred locations.

If you get in touch with undisturbed nature, it consists of some sacredness similar to that experienced by religious people. While there is no scientific explanation of how water is charged, it is strongly believed that different methods can be used. Charged water can be used specifically for energy healing. The other critical issue is that energy flows around us and not only inside, so when we interact with the environment or other people, energy flow is touched by that interaction.

Our state of health is determined by how freely the energy in our bodies can circulate and flow. While energy therapists are trained to detect the energy flows through their hands and create optimal conditions, hydrotherapy is a perfect method that can be used to ensure optimum energy flow.

This therapy can take place in a hydrotherapy pool consisting of charged water. You get into the pool to relax and enjoy an environment, and energy is at its optimum power while you are relaxing. However, you can feel some form of temporary discomfort in specific parts of the body while they are realigning. After the session in the hydrotherapy pool, you'll feel energized and refreshed. Water heals, and you can immediately feel its benefits once you move out of the pool.

You can also drink Reiki water, and it will provide healing powers. This water is used after a treatment session. You will often feel thirsty after the treatment. Many people feel the difference in their bodies during and after the treatment, which rebalances the energy system in your body. If you take a bath using charged water, you'll feel rejuvenated and energized.

If you are a novice in the world of Reiki healing, these are different tools you should know about. The items explained in this chapter can be used for various healing, so you should know your intention first. Make sure that all tools are charged or energized for the best results. When you use any tool for healing, make your intention known and always repeat it.

Conclusion

Reiki energy provides a unique healing power. Once you master this technique, you can help people through gentle touch. In this book, we have provided you with all the information you need to use your psychic power and start your journey as a psychic Reiki practitioner. We began this book by explaining the concept of Reiki, its principles, and its symbols. As a beginner, to give you the full experience, we made sure to include what takes place during a Reiki session.

To become a psychic Reiki practitioner, there are certain things to familiarize yourself with, such as energies, chakras, meditation, and visualization. We have dedicated two chapters in this book to provide you with everything you need to know about these four concepts. We have also included exercises and techniques so you can apply everything you have learned to yourself.

Having psychic abilities is a valuable gift. However, if you do not work on nurturing these abilities, you'll feel stuck and will lack the creativity to help others. Spiritual guides, clearing, and grounding can help improve your gift to be a better healer. We have also introduced the concept of the "Clairs" and how they can develop your psychic abilities, so you can expand on your intuition.

The second part of the book is mainly focused on healing. You can not heal others before first healing yourself. For this reason, we have included exercises to help you perform self-healing techniques. This is a vital skill every beginner should master before they start working with patients. We have provided a detailed explanation of how to connect with Reiki and draw from its energy. After healing yourself, you'll be ready to heal others. You will combine your psychic gift and your knowledge of Reiki to help them feel better.

We have also discussed using both telepathic and psychic abilities, so you can perform "distance healing" using various healing symbols and techniques. Psychics should have more than their regular eyes open. They should activate their third eye as well and journey into its temple. We have dedicated a whole chapter to activating the third eye temple and answering all the related questions, including how to activate your third eye chakra.

We ended the book by discussing all the tools a practitioner will need in their practice, like crystals, tarots, trinkets, and Reiki water. To help get you started, we have offered tips on how to use these tools and how to incorporate them into Reiki sessions.

By now, you have become familiar with the psychic Reiki topic. Use everything you have learned so far to heal others and yourself. Whenever you have a question or feel stuck with something, come back to this book, and you'll find an answer.

Part 2: Psychic Vampires

The Psychic Self-Defense Guide for Empaths and Highly Sensitive People Wanting Protection against Attacks on Their Energy

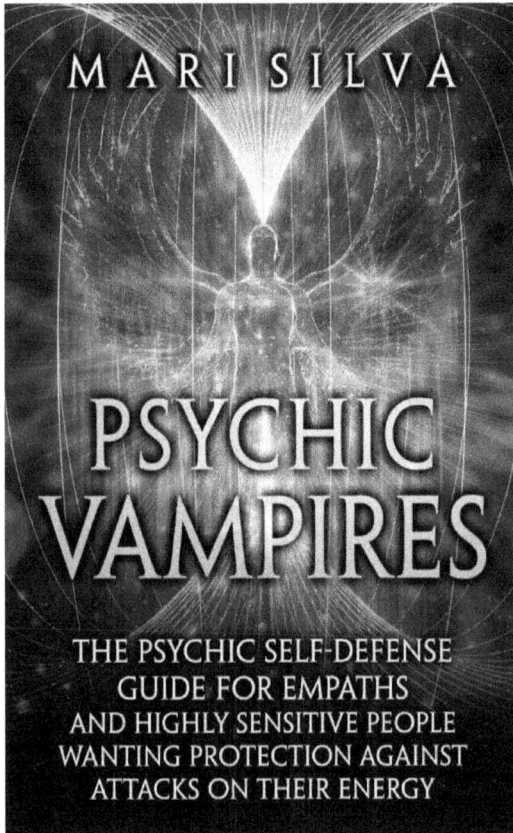

Introduction

You were completely fine. You were minding your own business or walking around, and then someone invaded your space. They were a co-worker, friend, family member, or even a complete stranger.

They came in, exchanged a few words with you, and then left as abruptly as they came in. After they left, you weren't the same.

Maybe you were happy, at peace, or even feeling like you feel on any normal day, just average. The only thing you know is that you were feeling fine, but you became completely overwhelmed after your encounter with them.

Now that you're alone again, you're feeling anxious, stressed, angry, sad, or any other negative emotions. You don't know why, how, or when you became this way, and you try, you really try so hard, but you can't seem to shake off this feeling.

If you try to rewind and focus, you'll be shocked to realize that they came into your space in a bad mood but left feeling better. So why is it you who is still struggling then?

If you've ever felt drained after talking to, interacting with, or even merely watching someone, then you've already felt what it's like to deal with a psychic vampire.

Psychic vampires are people who negatively affect other people's emotions, whether it's intentional or not. Their mere presence is enough to affect any normal person, so imagine how bad it would be if they were to invade the personal space of an empath or highly sensitive person.

The empath is a loving, kind-hearted, caring soul, and the highly sensitive person – an extremely perceptive, hyper-aware, and gentle spirit. The encounter will be toxic, to say the least.

That's why we decided to present you with this book. Here, you'll find everything you need to know about identifying and dealing with psychic vampires.

You'll get to know whether you're an empath or a highly sensitive person and the subtle differences between the two personality types. You'll know everything about how auras and energy work, and then you'll learn how to protect your boundaries from psychic vampires, recharge, and maintain a pristine and vibrant aura.

You'll probably find a myriad of books on the same topic on the market, but there's a reason this book is curated for you.

This book has been written in the simplest language. You won't struggle with any jargon or complicated phrases. It's a great place for beginners to understand themselves and learn how to take care of their energy.

You'll have everything you need to spot a psychic vampire and prevent them from tainting your energy by the end of this book. You'll get hands-on instruction, step-by-step guides, and scientifically proven methods and techniques to preserve your inner peace.

To end your journey through this book with a bang, we'll give you a 30-day challenge to protect your energy. You'll wake up every day and repeat strong affirmations, then check items and wellness exercises off the checkbox that you'll learn how to create.

Whatever made you struggle before won't be able to affect you as strongly anymore.

Now, it's time to create a healthier, more peaceful, and more vibrant version of yourself.

Chapter 1: Are You an Empath or a Highly Sensitive Person?

Empaths and highly sensitive people are everyone's go-to refuge whenever they're feeling down or need emotional support. Despite that, they're often misunderstood and misjudged, especially in highly competitive settings like the workplace.

Highly sensitive people are very perceptive.
https://unsplash.com/photos/0Pf7fKRtDPI

If you've often been told you're "too sensitive" or "too emotional," there are high chances you're either an empath or a highly sensitive person.

So, what does it mean to be either? Is there any difference between empaths and highly sensitive people? How can you know if you're one of them? You'll find the answers to all these questions in this chapter.

Who Is an Empath?

Whenever there's talk about empaths or highly sensitive people, it's easy to remember Dolly Parton's famous quote: *"If you see someone without a smile, you give them yours."*

This quote perfectly describes empaths. Empaths walk around with their hearts on their sleeves. They feel their sole purpose in life is to make others' lives better, so they take it upon themselves to try and solve other people's problems. This need to help others stems from their super-human ability to tune into other people's emotions.

Their ability extends way beyond the definition of empathy, which is the ability to understand other people's feelings. Not only do they read other people's feelings like open books, but they also absorb those emotions as if they were their own.

When empaths see sad people, they feel sad. When they encounter those who are angry, frustrated, depressed, or unhappy, they feel the same.

After years of research, science has confirmed the presence of what's dubbed now as "mirror neurons" inside empaths' brains. Their empathy allows them to see through other people's emotional states, and their mirror neurons enable them to mirror the states they witness.

In short, empaths are people who are highly sensitive to the emotional states of those around them. If that is the case for empaths, then what about highly sensitive people? Is it just another fancy title given to empaths? Not exactly.

Who Is a Highly Sensitive Person?

Like empaths, a highly sensitive person (HSP) is more sensitive than normal people. However, the way their sensitivity works is fundamentally different from that of an empath.

While empaths feel others deeply and mirror their emotions, HSPs have a heightened central nervous system that's extremely sensitive to external stimuli. They resonate with their surroundings, and it doesn't necessarily have to be from dealing with other people.

Their central nervous system is strongly stimulated by all kinds of environmental, physical, emotional, and social triggers. This phenomenon is scientifically described as having sensory processing sensitivity, or SPS.

HSPs are often disparaged in society for reacting "too strongly" or being "too sensitive." However, their highly sensitive nature gives them an unparalleled edge over others.

According to Dr. Elaine Aron and her colleagues, who have spent years researching HSPs, HSPs make up around 20% of the population. They summarized the characteristics of HSPs into four key aspects, denoted in the DOES acronym.

DOES refers to the following:

- **Depth of Processing**

  They can scan their environments and process the information they perceive at a terrifyingly accurate speed. It's a bit ironic then that they take a lot of time to respond to the stimuli, but that's only because they take a lot of time analyzing their surroundings and testing out the consequences of every possible course of action before they move.

- **Overstimulation**

  With their heightened ability to perceive and process information, it makes sense that they're easily overstimulated by the amount of data they absorb. Their sense of sound, touch, smell, vision, and taste is much more heightened than the normal person's, so much so that a normal daily routine can be overstimulating for them.

- **Emotional Reactivity or Empathy**

  The "E" in DOES can refer to emotional reactivity, which makes them react strongly to a stimulus, or experience empathy, which makes them feel others' emotions.

- **Sensing the Subtle**

  HSPs are akin to fine-tuned sensors. They can recognize subtle actions, like a person's body language, and understand their emotional state by analyzing those subtle cues.

Empaths vs. Highly Sensitive People

Many HSPs mistake themselves for empaths. Although both personality traits are close in nature to each other, empaths and HSPs aren't the same. There are as many similarities as there are differences between the two.

Let's take a closer look at both the similarities and differences between empaths and HSPs.

- **Similarities**

Empaths and HSPs both have a highly sensitive nature. They're both easily stimulated, need time alone to recharge, and are easily overwhelmed by crowds. They both enjoy getting lost in nature, have a rich inner world, and prefer peace and quiet over chaos and noise. Although it may be to a lesser degree, HSPs also enjoy lending a helping hand to others whenever they can.

- **Differences**

Most HSPs are introverted in nature, but empaths can be introverts or extroverts. That's why HSPs often need more downtime to recover from the aftermath of socializing or overstimulation.

Meanwhile, empaths take the heightened sensitivity of HSPs to a whole new level, as displayed by their ability to "mirror" others' feelings. This mirroring ability can be too strong to the extent they start showing the same physical symptoms they notice in others. For instance, they can blush when they see someone blushing or experience stomach aches when someone feels nauseous in front of them. That's not something HSPs experience.

Another differentiating trait is how empaths mistake others' emotions for their own. They're often unable to discern their own emotions from those of others, so they're often dyed with their companions' colors. That's why they may start behaving differently depending on the person they're hanging out with.

Finally, most empaths are strongly spiritual, but that's not necessarily the case with HSPs.

When you consider all their traits, empaths are usually highly sensitive people, not vice versa. This can be explained by the empathy spectrum, which goes as follows:

Empath-deficient personalities → Regular people → HSPs → Empaths

If empaths lie on the extreme right end of the spectrum, then narcissists (and those with antisocial personality disorders) lie on the extreme left end of the spectrum. Normal people lie in the middle, and HSPs have more empathy than normal people but fewer than empaths.

The Challenges of Living with High Sensitivity

Whether you're an empath or an HSP, living with high sensitivity can be extremely challenging. In the next chapter, we'll get into more depth about the challenges facing anyone living with a highly sensitive nature, but we'll take a good look here first.

Living with high sensitivity poses a myriad of challenges, including the following:

1. Easily feeling stimulated by their surroundings, other people, or daily life in general

2. Getting emotionally and physically burned out quickly

3. Feeling stressed out in crowded places

4. Often feeling as if no one understands them or that they don't fit in

5. Feeling the need to go into isolation to deal with the emotional or sensory overload

6. Having trouble setting boundaries or saying "no."

7. Feeling scared of intimacy and romantic relationships

8. Being easily influenced by others' emotions

9. Struggling with anxiety or depression

10. Trying so hard to avoid conflict

11. Being a harsh self-critic

The Traits of Empaths and Highly Sensitive People

Whether you're an empath or a highly sensitive person, you'll have the following defining characteristics:

1. You Have a Lot of Empathy

This goes without saying, but you're someone who deeply feels other people's emotions. As an HSP, you can instantly recognize how others feel, which makes you understand their thoughts to a certain extent. You take it further by mirroring their feelings and emotional states if you're an empath.

2. Your Gut Feeling Is Usually Right

Both empaths and HSPs have uncanny intuition that mostly turns out to be true. If you're either, you'll often have a gut feeling that something just isn't right, whether or not you can find the root of this feeling. This gut feeling helps you recognize when someone is being dishonest or if doing something will have negative consequences.

3. You Love Getting Lost in Nature

Many people love taking a break from their hectic lives to enjoy the serenity of nature, but empaths and HSPs feel attuned to nature whenever they stumble across it. While others brush away the beauty of nature during their stressful times, merely passing by plants or hearing the birds chirping can be enough to rejuvenate empaths and HSPs.

4. You Can't Stop Caring

Although this is more prominent in empaths, both personalities have trouble hiding their caring nature. Whenever an empath or an HSP comes across someone in distress, they feel responsible for alleviating their pain. The difference is that while HSPs can maintain their sense of self in these situations, empaths often absorb those feelings of distress and make them their own. Empaths also get deeply troubled and disappointed whenever they cannot provide help.

5. People Tend to Trust You with Their Problems

Thanks to your empathic nature, you're an excellent listener and supporter. That's one of the biggest reasons you find people trust you with their problems, even if they know you can't provide a solution. Merely talking with you makes them feel better.

6. You're Highly Attuned to the Surroundings

Although most empaths are only highly sensitive toward others' emotions, some share the HSPs' high sensitivity toward their surroundings. These empaths, like all HSPs, feel easily stimulated by fragrances, sounds, physical stimuli, and taste. All of these stimuli may even trigger emotional responses. Following a bout of strong stimulation, you need some time alone in a quiet environment to recharge.

7. The Way You See the World Is Unique

Empaths and HSPs see the world differently from those around them. Their ability to feel beyond what others do expands their experience, enriching their inner environment. Most artists, musicians, and creatives are either empaths or HSPs.

Famous Empaths and HSPs

We've had a lot of great empaths and HSPs throughout history. Like their polar opposites - the narcissists, Machiavellians, and psychopaths - empaths and HSPs have left their unique footprint on humanity. However, contrary to their polar opposites, their impact shines brightly.

Here are a few examples of famous empaths and HSPs:

1. Nelson Mandela

Nelson Mandela is a prominent historical figure known for sacrificing himself for the greater good. His strong intuition gave him the strength to fight for what he believed was right, and he sacrificed years of his life to achieve the freedom he longed for.

2. Oprah Winfrey

There's almost no one who doesn't love Oprah. She has grown in popularity thanks to how she used her empathic abilities to benefit others. She's always been a motherly figure who shone with a caring aura. Add to that her excellent ability to understand people, and there's no wonder everyone trusts and opens their hearts to her.

3. Mother Teresa

There are very few empaths who could achieve what Mother Teresa did. Although she spent her life caring for the sick and needy, she maintained her sense of stability throughout her journey.

Perhaps her beliefs as a devout Christian protected her from getting burned out. The more she gave to others, the more she could replenish her spirituality, and feeling close to God gave her what she needed to sustain her empathic energy.

4. Mahatma Gandhi

Mahatma Gandhi was the ultimate pacifist. He sacrificed years of his life fighting for what he believed in, just like Mandela. He also vowed to live a life of chastity and poverty, just like Mother Teresa.

His empathic nature left him vulnerable to the suffering of others, but he didn't close off his heart or suffer from overstimulation. Instead, he learned how to maintain the balance between feeling the pain caused by negative emotions and calming the soul to accept the suffering. As a result, his impact on the Indian people wasn't any less than that of Mother Teresa.

5. Nicole Kidman

Nicole Kidman described herself as a highly sensitive person, and she's the perfect example of how an HSP can leverage their abilities to pursue a successful, self-fulfilling career. After all, acting is all about perfectly portraying the characters' emotions.

Kidman stayed true to her empathic nature by pursuing philanthropic work and charity in her personal life. She became a UNICEF ambassador and was later recognized as a "Citizen of the World" by the UN.

6. George Orwell

You can't imagine George Orwell as the type of guy to be empathic, although his nature did seep into his work. In his own way, Orwell did everything he could to battle colonialism.

There was even a time when he felt the need to take his empathy to a level few others could reach. He wanted to understand people's misery on a deeper level, so he disguised himself as a beggar on the streets of London and lived there for a while.

7. Dolly Parton

It can be hard to imagine someone as outgoing and vibrant as Dolly Parton as an empath, much less an HSP. However, she is a true example of how highly sensitive people have an amazingly rich inner environment that others rarely get to have.

Throughout her career as a songwriter, Dolly maintained an open heart and the ability to stay true to herself. It's hard to imagine from a bystander's point of view, but any HSP can feel how much of a remarkable feat that is.

In her latest book, Dolly Parton, Songteller: My Life in Lyrics, she wrote, "*As a songwriter and as a person, I have to leave myself wide open. I suffer a lot because I am so open. I hurt a lot, and when I hurt, I hurt all over because I cannot harden my heart to protect myself. I always say that I strengthen the muscles around my heart, but I can't harden them.*"

Test Yourself: Are You an Empath or an HSP?

Based on everything you've read in this chapter, you may strongly feel you're either an HSP or an empath. Here's a self-quiz to help you better identify your personality.

Empathy Quiz

Check all the statements you feel to be true.

1. You're often told you're shy, overly sensitive, or introverted.

2. You frequently feel anxious or overwhelmed.

3. Arguing with others, or hearing others argue, makes you feel ill.

4. You often feel like you don't belong.

5. Crowded places overwhelm you.

6. Noise, strong odor, and talkative people overstimulate you.

7. You can't tolerate scratchy clothes or are overly sensitive toward chemicals.

8. You prefer to drive your own car so you can leave anytime.

9. Whenever you're feeling stressed, you overeat.

10. Intimate relationships make you feel suffocated.

11. You get easily startled.

12. You react strongly to caffeine or certain medications.

13. You have low pain tolerance.

14. You feel the need to isolate yourself from people.

15. You easily absorb other people's emotions, stress, and sometimes even physical symptoms.

16. The idea of multitasking overwhelms you – you prefer doing one thing at a time.

17. Being in nature rejuvenates you.

18. You need a long time to recover after meeting with energy vampires.

19. You prefer small cities to large ones.

20. You prefer one-on-one interactions to large gatherings.

Your Score

- 1 to 5 statements: mild empathic tendencies
- 6 to 10: moderate empathic tendencies
- 11 to 15: strong empathic tendencies
- 15 to 20: true empath

High Sensitivity Quiz

Again, check all the statements you find to be true:

1. You're easily overwhelmed by sensory triggers.

2. You're hyper-aware of any subtle changes in your environment.

3. You're easily affected by other people's moods.

4. You have extremely low pain tolerance.

5. Whenever you're going through a busy day, you feel the need to isolate yourself in a dark room, a quiet corner, on your bed, or in any private place to escape from stimulation.

6. Caffeine, in particular, makes you more sensitive.

7. Bright lights, coarse fabrics, sirens, strong smells, and other strong stimuli easily overwhelm you.

8. You have a rich and complex inner environment.

9. You enjoy and are deeply moved and inspired by arts and music.

10. Loud noises make you uncomfortable.

11. Your nervous system often gets too overwhelmed, so you take some time out to be alone.

12. You have strong principles and moral values.

13. You get startled easily.

14. You get overwhelmed when you need to do many things in a short time.

15. You instantly recognize what needs to be fixed when people are uncomfortable in their physical environment.

16. You get annoyed when people egg you on to do many things at once.

17. You try hard to avoid making mistakes or forgetting things.

18. You avoid watching violent movies and shows.

19. Sometimes, you get unpleasantly aroused when you're overwhelmed by what's happening around you.

20. You get hangry – angry when hungry.

21. Any changes to your routine disturb you.

22. You go out of your way to arrange your life so you can avoid unpleasant situations or environments.

23. You get so nervous when someone is watching you perform a task that you often do so much worse than if you were alone.

24. Your parents and teachers often described you as sensitive or shy when you were a kid.

Your Score

If you've checked more than 14 of the previous statements, there is a high chance that you're an HSP. You may also be an HSP if you've checked fewer statements yet felt them too strongly.

Keep in mind that the results of these quizzes should only help you understand yourself better. They're by no means a definitive answer or a basis to build your life upon.

To describe it briefly, empaths are people with extremely high emotional sensitivity, while highly sensitive people have a general sense of heightened sensitivity. However, that also means that both empaths and HSPs are highly attuned to the subtle changes in their surroundings. This ability often leaves them vulnerable to negative energy, especially when encountering others who leech off their empathic nature.

In the next chapter, we'll go into deeper detail about the struggles empaths and HSPs face in their daily lives.

Chapter 2: The Struggles of High Sensitivity

High sensitivity is a topic that doesn't garner a lot of awareness or attention. For this reason, there are many common misconceptions about high sensitivity and those who struggle with it. Many people don't realize that being highly sensitive goes far beyond feeling too deeply about one's emotions or taking everything to heart.

A highly sensitive individual has a heightened central nervous sensitivity to numerous stimuli, including social, physical, and emotional activities. Besides being more emotionally sensitive than the average person, an HSP also has a lower pain tolerance and can be irritated by seemingly normal social and environmental stimuli, such as large crowds, physical interactions, bright lights, and loud sounds. HSPs are often mistakenly and negatively labeled as "too dramatic," "overly sensitive," or "very quirky." This is why HSPs and non-HSPs don't realize that high sensitivity accompanies a wide range of strengths and positive traits despite the challenges. Most highly sensitive individuals believe that they're all alone and that no one truly understands their struggle. If you can relate to this, then you may find peace in knowing that around 20% of the general population is highly sensitive.

Being a highly sensitive person is not a condition you need to diagnose. It is simply a personality trait that prompts heightened responses to certain stimuli. If you took the quiz in the previous chapter, you already probably have a good idea of where you lie on the high sensitivity spectrum.

Highly sensitive people are often wrongly described as introverts and vice versa. It's important to note that while both personality traits share common characteristics, they are both very different. This confusion and the lack of awareness around high sensitivity can make it hard for HSPs to understand themselves fully.

This chapter explores what it means to be a highly sensitive individual in-depth. Here, you'll learn more about potentially triggering situations, which can help you identify the things that set off your reactivity. You'll also come across some examples of common struggles HSPs experience in their day. Finally, you'll find some mindfulness techniques to help you overcome these difficulties and protect your energy.

Highly Sensitive People in a Nutshell

Being a highly sensitive person comes with a lot of strengths and weaknesses. If you're an HSP, you're undoubtedly aware of the challenges this personality trait puts you in. However, you may be surprised to learn that your heightened sensitivity can also put you at an advantage in many of your social, professional, and romantic relationships.

When you're this sensitive, you can't help but feel offended by people's subtle actions or words, even when they genuinely mean no harm. You are likely to overreact to daily events and situations that are otherwise perceived as normal. Non-major issues in relationships can also greatly stress you out. Unfortunately, constantly being told that you're unreasonable and that your reactions are way out of proportion can cause you to question your own sanity. To get this out of the way, you're not delusional, and yes, your feelings are valid. Even if you don't necessarily react as others do, you perceive negative stressors more easily and intensely than others. Although negative experiences affect you on a deeper level, this is not a sign of weakness.

One of the downsides of being a highly sensitive person is that you tend to miss out on many social and professional experiences and opportunities. This is because you avoid situations that make you feel stressed and overwhelmed. Situations that give rise to feelings of discomfort, such as violence and conflict, can significantly affect you.

However, this means that you are also very affected and touched by the positive aspects of life. Music, beauty, art, and nature can move you deeply. In the best way possible, you feel emotional when witnessing touching events. This gives you the ability to find beauty in all your surroundings, but it also grants you exceptional intrapersonal skills. Being an HSP allows you to empathize with others and truly feel their emotions. You build great bonds and relationships with those around you, and the way you care for them makes you an indispensable friend. Even though HSPs are very soft-hearted and emotional, they are far from naive. Their empathic skills allow them to sense toxicity from miles away. They can always tell when something doesn't sit right, which is why they're very meticulous about who they let into their circle.

All of these characteristics make HSPs generally appreciative and grateful. They are thankful for their lives and know how to cherish the small pleasures of life, whether it's a fine meal or a mesmerizing piece of art. This is a very important quality that many people lack. The key to finding happiness and maintaining balance in life as an HSP lies in learning to manage and use your special attributes. This is how you channel your weaknesses into strengths. To do that, you need to fully grasp the challenges life offers. You may not realize as an HSP that while your pitfalls are intensely low, your highs can be extremely high.

Potential Triggers

Like everyone else, HSPs feel stressed when they come face to face with challenges and difficult situations. They are often aggravated by situations that others may not pay much attention to. Whenever they walk into a room, they notice subtleties, such as hostile behaviors or mild tension. This is why social gatherings and settings can be especially taxing for highly sensitive people. The following are some things that can be overwhelming to an HSP:

Busy Schedules

While some people work best under pressure and feel a sense of accomplishment and fulfillment when they have busy schedules to keep up with, having a hectic schedule is certainly not an HSP's cup of tea. A busy life will keep a highly sensitive individual on edge. It would be a recipe for constant stress. Highly sensitive individuals don't like having much to do in a limited timeframe, even if they know that they have plenty of time to do it. They can't help but feel overburdened with the possibility of not being able to find a way to make it work.

What to do: If you find yourself stuck with a busy schedule that you need to follow, then make sure to add positive experiences to your to-do list. Do something fun or indulge in a relaxing activity every day. You can go for a long walk in nature, paint, exercise, do yoga, or partake in any other activity that puts your mind at ease. This way, you can relieve some of the pressure. Try to free your mind of all the things you have to do during this time of day. Treat this positive activity as you would any other serious endeavor. Direct all your focus and attention to it.

Having Expectations to Meet

As empaths, highly sensitive individuals effortlessly pay extra attention to the emotions and needs of those around them. Because they automatically pick up on these things and worry about disappointing others. For this reason, HSPs find it especially hard to say no to other people. Feeling the dismay of others doesn't make it any easier for them. Additionally, HSPs are usually very self-critical. They also hold themselves accountable for the way other people feel. They believe that it's their duty to make other people happy, which is a burdensome responsibility to take on.

What to do: Other people's happiness and emotions are not your responsibility. One of the reasons you may feel inclined to take care of others is that you struggle with putting your own needs first. It helps to remember that when you compromise your own needs for other people's happiness, you'll feel resentful. You'll also burn yourself out and will not be able to help others the way you would like to anymore. If being helpful makes you happy, you need to maintain a balance between caring for yourself and others. You can't pour from an empty cup. Learn to become comfortable with setting boundaries for all your relationships. You also need to practice saying no when your own needs and wants are in question.

Conflicts

Everyone undoubtedly finds conflicts very stressful, especially with people they love and care about. However, for HSPs, conflicts can be extremely distressing. Many highly sensitive people avoid important conversations to avoid potential disagreements. When they feel saddened or disappointed by the actions of others, HSPs avoid speaking up because they're worried about creating problems. This creates a huge communication gap, which compromises an HSP's relationships.

As we mentioned above, highly sensitive people are also quick to catch subtleties and can immediately notice whenever someone is feeling slightly off. The problem here is that many HSPs immediately assume that the other person is angry with them. In most cases, they misinterpret other people's unrelated behaviors as a sign of oncoming conflict. This may cause them to avoid these people for no reason at all.

What to do: As an empath, you care deeply for others. It would also undoubtedly hurt you to lose important people in your life. This is why you have to be able to communicate your feelings and concerns with others. If you have healthy relationships with others, they will hear you out and be sure to avoid actions or behaviors that upset you rather than spiral into an argument. When you feel that someone acts differently from how they usually do, you shouldn't jump to conclusions. Instead, you need to communicate your concerns. This way, you'll be able to tell if this shift in behavior has anything to do with you.

Low Levels of Tolerance

We all have different tolerance levels and are likely to experience energy drains when we are met with certain experiences or events during the day. What drains someone's energy may not necessarily impact another person. To a highly sensitive person, any type of distraction can be detrimental. HSPs can get easily agitated and distracted whenever there are strong smells, loud noises, or bright lights. They can find it hard to relax whenever something exceeds their comfort levels.

Highly sensitive individuals may not appreciate surprises because they easily throw them off. They may also have low pain thresholds and can find it hard to tolerate hunger or thirst. While these are seemingly small stressors, they can become extremely frustrating for an HSP when they add up.

What to do: Since you can't always control your environment, especially in a public setting, you need to set up a safe space for yourself at home. Social interactions and the general environment can be very overwhelming for you. This is why you need to be able to recharge when you get home. Make sure that your home is soothing enough for your needs. Keep your home organized if mess stresses you out. Keep the lights dimmed and switch traditional clocks for digital ones if the ticking sounds annoy you. Staying on top of your home's maintenance needs will also ensure that appliances perform at optimal function (no buzzing or squeaking sounds). This way, you'll not have to worry about scheduling repairs. If you're sensitive to particular textures, make sure you eliminate them from your home. You can decorate your house with beautiful artwork, play relaxing movies, and use calming scented candles.

Failure

As you know, highly sensitive people are overly self-critical. This makes them highly introspective and self-doubtful. HSPs find it hard to let go of their mistakes. They keep rethinking embarrassing incidents or situations that appear to be incompetent. They stress over these minor failures more than the average individual would. Highly sensitive individuals don't like to be watched or assessed when doing something. Situations like these, such as public speaking events, competitions, or presentations, can make them feel very anxious. They are also likely to mess up because of how pressured and worried they feel. HSPs are characterized by their perfectionist tendencies and their need to get everything right.

What to do: Remember that mistakes are the perfect opportunities for growth and development. When lamenting over the past, try to remind yourself that you're probably the only person who noticed. If you're worried about an upcoming situation, think of the worst thing that can happen. So what does it matter if you forget a couple of words during your presentation, mess up during your speech, or fail to score a ranking in your sports competition? You'll have plenty of chances to make up for your mistakes. Besides, you're probably the only one who will remember these mishaps. Every once in a while, intentionally perform below your standards. Color outside the lines, don't make your bed in the morning or make changes to a recipe that you have spent months trying to master. Accept that not everything has to be perfect all the time.

General Tip: If you still don't know how to cope with certain stimuli, it's best if you avoid them altogether. Know the things that trigger you and take measures to avoid them. For instance, if you feel overwhelmed in crowded areas, run your errands early in the morning. If physical interactions make you agitated, sit far away from your touchy friends. If you find loud sounds unbearable, make sure that you have your earphones on you to listen to music whenever you need to. Don't watch thrillers, violent movies or videos, read things, or listen to songs that will make you feel bad.

Practicing Meditation and Mindfulness

Practicing meditation techniques improves life quality.
https://pixabay.com/images/id-1851165

As an HSP, you need to learn to set boundaries to improve your life quality. You can do so by practicing mindfulness and meditation techniques. These activities can help you understand how you feel toward certain life experiences. Meditation allows you to observe your emotions and thoughts through a wider lens. Over time, you'll be able to calm your body more easily and effectively. This will help you recover quickly from your stress and anxiety. These activities will also teach you to disengage from the things that overwhelm you so intense emotions do not overtake you.

You can do these exercises whenever you feel anxious about an upcoming event or gathering. If you're overwhelmed by a certain stimulus, break away from the situation and choose one of the following activities to do. This will help you regain your composure to return to the situation with a clearer and more positive mind. Incorporating these exercises into your daily routine can also help you deal with your high sensitivity more efficiently in the long run. They make great emotional and thought management techniques.

Mindfulness Exercises

Reset Your Awareness. The modern-day world is very demanding and incredibly fast-paced. To keep up, we all forget to pay attention to our surroundings. You can benefit greatly from taking the time to fully engage yourself in the surrounding environment. Connect with nature and indulge in life experiences with all your senses. Observe nature's different hues and colors, touch the dewy leaves, smell the flowers, and hear the chirping birds. Savor your meals and take the time to identify all the flavors. Make eating a feast for your eyes and enjoy the inviting smell.

Be Fully Present. Be entirely attentive to everything you do. Make sure you experience the joys in even the simplest activities.

Practice Self-Acceptance and Compassion. Whenever you catch yourself being overly critical of yourself, ask yourself if this is how you would treat a good friend of yours.

Bring Awareness to Your Breathing. Whenever you feel overwhelmed or overtaken by negative thoughts, sit down comfortably and close your eyes. Take a deep breath and bring awareness to the rhythm and pattern of your breathing. Inhale deeply and exhale fully.

Meditative Activities

Sitting Meditation: Sit down on a chair with your back straight and your feet resting flat on the floor. Keep your hands in your lap and breathe through your nose. Pay complete attention to how your breaths flow in and out of your body. Keep doing this for 3 to 5 minutes. If an intrusive thought or physical sensation interrupts your practice, don't try to resist it. Instead, acknowledge it and then imagine it floating away like a cloud. Return your awareness to your breath.

Body Scan Meditation: Lie down on your back. Keep your legs extended and flat on the floor, and place your hands beside you with your palms factoring upward. Slowly and intentionally direct your awareness to the different parts of your body. You can either start from your head and work down to your toes or do it the other way around. Take notice of any emotions, physical sensations, or thoughts regarding the body part you're focusing on.

Meditative Walks: Find a quiet place to conduct this meditation. It should be around 10 to 20 feet long. Walk slowly and focus your attention on the entire experience. Notice how your feet feel on the ground and all the physical sensations you experience while standing. Be aware of even the smallest movements that allow you to maintain your balance. When you get to the end of the room or pathway, turn around and do the same thing on your way back.

Being highly sensitive is often viewed as a negative personality trait. However, not many people realize that HSPs can excel in numerous areas in life with the right management techniques. To learn to deal with your high sensitivity, you must first identify your stressors.

Chapter 3: Auras and Energies

An aura is an electromagnetic spectrum formed due to an electromagnetic field that surrounds your body. Wait, what? An electromagnetic field produced by your body? It is hard to believe, but humans indeed radiate a low level of electricity, which we usually associate with an electromagnetic field. But how is this possible? Every body of matter is made up of tiny atoms, whether it's inanimate objects or living beings. From a physics perspective, your body is made up of a great number of atoms that form one uniform whole. Now, an atom consists of the nucleus, which contains protons and neutrons, whereas the outer region of an atom contains electrons and mostly empty space. So, in essence, an atom is merely an empty space with a charge. Each atom has an electromagnetic field, which repels or attracts it to other atoms.

An aura is an electromagnetic field.
https://www.pexels.com/photo/light-woman-art-relaxation-6931816

These atoms come together to form your body, and their electromagnetic field keeps your body from merging into other matter. This electromagnetic field is associated with the energy a person might exude. On the other hand, the spectrum formed as a result of this electromagnetic field is considered a person's aura. The atoms present in your body vibrate at a different wavelength than other bodies. We can't see this vibration because it happens at an atomic level. That results in an electromagnetic spectrum of various colors that make up your aura. Think of it like this. Your aura is like a halo around you, which can be felt by people when they're in your presence, although not visible to everyone. The aura is also seen as a protective shield for your physical body.

Relationship between Aura Mind, Body, and Spirit

Every person's aura embodies their personality, mood, and spirituality. It contains all the negative and positive energies within your mind and body, and the dominant out of these dictates the type of aura that will be generated. The electromagnetic spectrum that makes up an aura usually consists of seven layers associated with a particular chakra along the spine. Each chakra is identified by the color associated with it.

A person with a healthy aura signifies a healthy body, mind, and spirit. For instance, if a person is filled with negative emotions of rage, jealousy, and anger, the energy of their aura will probably signify the same thing. In contrast, a person with warm and happy feelings will have a calm aura that attracts people toward them. The same concept can be applied to physical ailments. People with health conditions will have an unhealthy aura, whereas a healthy aura will emanate positive energy. People who can read auras can thus predict if a person is in good health or not.

Seven Chakras and Auric Bodies

The seven chakras.
https://pixabay.com/images/id-6513344

The different layers of the electromagnetic spectrum that make up a person's aura are also commonly known as subtle bodies. These layers are often associated with the seven energy chakras of the human body. Each layer is close together and is affected by a person's thoughts, health, talents, life potential, and even past lives or karmic lessons. Thus, the color of your aura is subject to change according to these different factors. The seven energy chakras are associated with the seven layers of Aura, or subtle bodies, in the following sequence:

1. Root Chakra/Etheric Body

The root chakra is considered to be your life force energy and is located at the base of the spine. It is often associated with the color red as it controls activities related to the heart and blood. The root chakra is associated with the first layer that makes up your aura: the etheric body. This layer is the closest to your physical body and is composed of bluish-white thin energy lines in color. This color usually varies from light blue to deep blue for a healthy and happy person.

2. Sacral Chakra/Emotional Body

The Sacral chakra, also known as the orange or splenic center, is the energy center for your feelings and emotions. Located near the lower abdomen, the sacral chakra is associated with orange color and controls your emotions. It is associated with the emotional body layer of your aura, which is directly above the etheric body. This layer expresses the full spectrum of your emotions in a cloud-like aura, extending three to four inches from your body. Like your emotions, this layer has a varying range of colors and often changes with changes in emotions.

3. Solar Plexus Chakra/Mental Body

The solar plexus chakra is located near the stomach and controls your mental energy. It is represented by the color yellow and is associated with the auric layer of the mental body. This layer contains your thoughts and ideas, creative side, and mental processes. Many people consider this layer to be a second brain where thoughts are processed. This layer makes up a bright yellow light radiating from your head that moves along tithe rest of your body.

4. Heart Chakra/Astral Body

The heart chakra is connected with your emotional energy, and it is located at the very center of the human body. It connects all the upper and lower chakras together and encompasses complex emotions and issues related to the heart. Thus, it is said to be the bridge between the emotional and physical planes. This chakra is associated with the astral body and is represented by a beautiful rainbow color. When a person is in love, this layer of their aura is especially prominent and akin to fireworks.

5. Throat Chakra/Etheric Template

Located at the throat, the throat chakra regulates your communication energy and is often associated with the color blue. The throat chakra is associated with the etheric template layer of the aura, which is used to indicate the physical blueprint of your body. Thus, this layer can be used to predict physical ailments or illnesses.

6. Third Eye Chakra/Celestial Body

The third eye chakra connects to the celestial body layer and is often represented by a dark blue color. This chakra is located right between the eyes and is associated with spiritual connection and understanding. It represents your ability to focus on what really matters. The celestial body consists of spiritual and mental functions, including emotions, thoughts, disturbances, and energy manifestation.

7. Crown Chakra/Casual Body

The crown chakra is located at the top of the head and extends upward. It is represented by either violet or indigo. This layer vibrates at the highest frequency and therefore protects all other layers of your aura. This layer is usually seen as a brilliant white color on the most external side of your aura.

HSPs and Aura Reading

As a highly sensitive person, you've probably experienced a very strong sense of what's about to happen or just predicted people's moods and energies simply by looking at them. The thing about being a highly sensitive person (HSP) is that you can experience things on a different frequency to others. This is why it's so easy for a highly sensitive person to read a person's aura. Because their brain is wired differently, HSPs have an enhanced sense of emotions, both theirs and those coming from others. When vibrating at a higher frequency than regular people, HSPs pick up the aura a person is emanating.

For instance, an HSP will be able to feel the tension between a couple, even when they're behaving completely normally. Similarly, an HSP will be able to sense trouble, doom, or sadness coming from someone dealing with an illness, whether physical or mental. Some highly sensitive people also claim to be able to see the different colored aura exuding from a person. In this case, it's better if you understand what each color of an aura represents since each color has a different meaning.

1. Red Aura

The color red is often associated with the root chakra and hence with the heart and blood. Different shades of red symbolize different emotions and characteristics of a person:

- Light red - symbolizes sensual feelings, grounded emotions, and feelings of energy.

- Dark red - represents strong will, realistic personality, and stubbornness.

- Bright pink - often considered the color of love, is associated with kindness, love, and affection.

- Muddy red - toward the darker shades of red and hence symbolize rage, anger, feelings of anxiety, and unforgiving nature.

2. Orange Aura

Orange color is associated with the sacral chakra, which controls emotions, creativity, and fertility. Mainly, two shades of orange are produced in auras:

- Bright orange - is associated with courage, creativity, and an outgoing, extroverted personality.

- Dark orange - inclined toward darker emotions like addiction, stress, lack of motivation, or ambition.

3. Yellow Aura

Connected to the solar plexus chakra, or solar energy, the yellow aura is associated with life force, ego, and wellness. It can be visible in shades of:

- Bright Gold – Connected with feelings of spiritual awakening, divine protection, and enlightenment.

- Pale yellow – corresponds to a playful, easy-going, and optimistic personality and spiritual clarity.

- Muddy yellow – a darker shade of yellow, usually due to stress or fatigue.

- Bright yellow – Associated with a self-centered and controlling personality.

4. Green Aura

Green is connected to the heart chakra, and the aura represents kindness, compassion, and growth. It is usually visible in shades of:

- Light green – symbolizes creativity, love, and compassion.

- Dark green – represents an empathetic and soothing personality, as well as a healing nature.

- Muddy green – darker emotion, concerned with feelings of resentment, jealousy, and insecurity.

5. Blue Aura

Corresponding to the throat chakra, the blue aura relates to truthfulness, communication, and expression. It is visible in the following shades.

- Light blue – is associated with feelings of peace and a truthful personality.

- Dark blue – symbolizes open-mindedness and deep spiritual awareness.

- Muddy blue – is associated with fear of the future and hiding things.

6. Purple Aura

Associated with the third eye chakra, the purple aura is concerned with wisdom, spirituality, and intuition. It has shades of:

- White and Violet – feelings of intense healing, wisdom, and meditative nature.

- Indigo – is associated with wisdom, intuition, and integrity.

- Violet – is concerned with feelings of healing and responsibility.

7. Silver Aura

Usually present in overlapping waves with other colors and represents intense emotions. Visible in shades of:

- Bright silver – represents a nurturing personality and intuitive nature.

- Muddy gray – indicate underlying health issues.

- Dark gray or black – symbolizes energy blocks or feelings of suppressed grief.

How to Read Your Aura

Before you can start reading your own aura, it's better to understand what an aura or electromagnetic field looks like. To do this, choose a random colorful object and place it against a neutral background. Allow your vision to get fuzzy and softened before focusing it on the object. You'll start to see a blurred-out color surrounding the object, which is the object's aura. Practice this technique with objects as much as possible, and then move on to plants. Plants have a more distinct aura compared to inanimate objects. Once you've practiced this enough, it's time to start to read your own aura.

To read your aura, stand in front of a mirror, and focus on a certain part of your body, preferably your hands. Rub your hands together, slowly move them apart, and then bring them back together. While you do this, soften your vision, and see if you observe a distinct color around your hands. Once you've noticed this color, it will become more distinct, and you'll be able to observe it all around your body. You may even notice different colors mixed together.

How to Read Someone Else's Aura

Reading someone else's aura is much like reading your own, and HSPs usually have pretty good instincts about the process. To read someone else's aura, all you need to do is, ask your subject to stand against a neutral background. Focus on the person's nose, but not too deeply. Make sure you keep your vision relaxed while also focusing on your peripheral vision. This way, even though your eyes will be focused on the subject's nose, you'll also be able to observe the person's sides. After a while, you'll start to observe a benign outline being formed along the person's sides. Now, through your peripheral vision, you need to start observing the outline, and you'll notice it grow stronger. Finally, bring your eyes from the subject's nose to their forehead to better view their aura.

How to Differentiate between Your Aura and Someone Else's

Empaths and highly sensitive people often confuse other people's feelings and aura with their own. This is mainly because of their ability to feel others' emotions intensely that they misunderstand them for their own feelings. However, this can sometimes be draining for HSPs, and they should be able to tell the difference between their own aura and energy versus that of other people. To do this, follow these tips:

- When you're getting overwhelmed with emotions and negative energy, take a moment to breathe and calm down.
- Now, ask yourself if you're really feeling a certain way or if you're channeling someone else's energy.
- Observe your emotions and take a few moments to think before you answer the above question.
- After a while, you'll find that the negative aura you felt was not your own but that of another person in your proximity, possibly someone you care about.
- So, instead of letting yourself get overwhelmed, get into a peaceful mindset, and try to help your friend or loved one through their problem.

While there's no concrete scientific evidence backing up the existence of auras, many people have experienced this phenomenon. A person's aura can tell us many things about them, their feelings, their personality, and even hidden emotions. However, as a highly sensitive person, it's also important that you take care of yourself and learn where to draw the line when it comes to empathy. Whether you're an HSP or not, boundaries are the most important part of living a healthy life.

Chapter 4: Identifying Toxic Energies

Empaths and highly sensitive people should learn how to identify toxic energy to avoid it. Unfortunately, there isn't an app on your phone that notifies you when you're around negative people. Toxic energy is all about the negativity that is apparent in a person's feelings and actions. For instance, someone who is jealous, angry, and who isn't satisfied with their life will always try to put you down and will never be able to celebrate your successes or be happy for you. They may even make you feel bad when you share your good news with them because they are consumed with jealousy and anger.

People who possess toxic energy are a destructive force to themselves and everyone around them. It consumes and devours them from the inside. It takes hold of them, and they are unable to control it. This toxicity reveals itself in actions that can hurt and even destroy the people in their lives. That said, not all toxic people are aware that they emit this kind of energy, but that still doesn't make them or their actions any less harmful.

Whether positive or negative, Energies are felt, especially if you are an empath or a highly sensitive person. For this reason, the best way to identify toxic energy is by how you feel when you are around certain people. Their negativity is like a vacuum or a vampire that sucks your energy. After spending time around these people, you feel drained and in a bad mood. Even if they don't display toxic behavior, the energy and bad vibes they emit can negatively impact your mood and your psyche. As an

HSP, you'll be able to sense things that most people can't, and it can affect you more than others. You may not even be aware of it, especially if the person you are around doesn't usually show any negative or toxic traits. All you know is that you feel worse and drained every time you are around certain people.

How Can You Identify Toxic Energies?

In addition to feeling worse and drained after spending time around toxic energy, there are certain behaviors you need to look out for to protect yourself from energy vampires.

They Complain All the Time

They often complain about everything and everyone. They are so consumed with toxic energy that they cannot see the good, and they only focus on the negative. Even if everything is fine, they will find something to complain about.

It Is Never Their Fault

They are always the victim, either of their circumstances or of someone else. Nothing is ever their fault. They will never self-reflect to see if they may be at fault. It is always someone else.

They Always Criticize

Since they only focus on the negative, they will always criticize you, their friends, other people, or anything they lay their eyes on. Their constant criticism, just like their constant complaining, creates an air of negativity that can affect your mood and make you feel horrible every time you are around them.

That said, they don't handle criticism very well. Even if it is constructive criticism or you want to point out how their actions hurt your feelings. They will feel attacked, offended, and will get very angry as a result.

They Will Bring You Down

As mentioned above, negative people are incapable of being happy for you or anyone else. If you share exciting news with them, they will find a way to bring you down. For instance, if you get promoted and share the news with them, instead of being happy for you, they may say something like, "This should have happened years ago" or "They are clearly promoting anyone now." They are miserable people who want to make everyone feel like them. They take the saying "misery loves company" to the next level.

Consider Your Feelings

One of the surest ways to identify toxic energies is to consider your feelings toward this person. Do you get anxious every time you know you'll meet them? Does their name showing up on your phone screen ruin your mood? Do you dread having a conversation with them? Listen to your gut feeling. Even if this person doesn't exhibit any of the traits we have mentioned above, you should still follow your instinct. You are an empath, so you are most likely onto something if you sense bad vibes.

These people only focus on the negative. They are unable to see the positive in anything or anyone. They are unhappy individuals who keep spreading negativity wherever they go. Take a look at the people in your life. Is there someone – after spending time with them – that leaves you feeling drained?? Do you have a friend who makes you feel less happy or excited about life after you talk to them? Even if other people don't feel the same as an HSP, toxic energies easily affect you. For this reason and for the sake of your mental health and well-being, you should learn how to protect yourself from these energies.

How Can You Protect Yourself from Toxic Energies?

It isn't an exaggeration to say that you should be over-protective of your energy. Toxic energies have a huge impact on empaths and HSP. Protecting your energy will pave the way toward building a resilient psychic defense. When you are always surrounded by negativity, your psyche and mental health will be vulnerable. Additionally, being around toxic people will leave you exposed to them. They will drain your energy and make you consumed with negativity.

Once you recognize the source of negativity in your life, you should set boundaries with these people to protect yourself from their toxicity. This will give you your power back as you'll not give them the chance to "suck your energy" anymore. Learning how to protect your energy is vital for your well-being and mental health.

Setting Boundaries

One of the best pieces of advice we can give an HSP is setting boundaries. Negative people enjoy throwing pity parties for themselves, but you don't have to accept the invitation every time. As mentioned, they love complaining and spreading negativity. However, you don't have to be a part of their drama. Distance yourself from these people. Setting boundaries isn't always easy, but it is vital, so we will discuss it in detail in the next chapters.

Don't React to Their Negativity

Energy vampires always want to get a reaction from you. It is very easy to react to negativity. For instance, if someone yells at you, you'll react in the same way by getting angry and raising your voice. It is human nature to react to negative situations instantly and without thinking. It is an impulse to protect ourselves and our egos. When you interact with a negative person, it is best to respond instead of reacting.

Simply put, be the bigger person. If they yell, call you names, or criticize you, take a moment to either respond calmly or simply walk away. Choosing the high road will prevent you from stooping to their level and allowing them to drain your energy. This will also help you stay in control of your emotions and the situation.

Understand You Can't Change Them

You can't change people. This is a fact you need to understand to save and protect your energy. Don't stick around, hoping they will change someday as they won't. As a result of your sensitive nature, you may find it hard to walk away from someone, especially if they are close friends or family. In this case, you can try and talk to them to help them understand how their actions are affecting you. However, if they still act the same way, then you need to walk away. Waiting for them to change will do no good to either of you.

You need your energy to be able to take care of yourself, your work, your life, and the people you care about. If you let these people keep draining you because you hope they will change one day, this will affect all other areas of your life. Avoid arguing or contradicting them, hoping they will see things from your perspective because they won't. This will only make them more stubborn, and you'll feel as if you are talking to a brick wall which can be very frustrating.

If you must interact with energy vampires, don't exert your energy. If they are complaining, let them. Don't tell them that things aren't that bad or that they should focus on the positive. Don't give them your opinion or advice. Just keep the conversation flowing by giving short answers like "Really?" "Oh, that's so bad" "How did that happen?" This way, you preserve your energy and let your negative friend vent.

Discuss Lighter Topics

Energy vampires crave drama. To protect your own energy, don't give them a chance to start complaining or criticizing. If they start negatively by talking about how horrible their job or their life is, try to change the subject. Ask them if they have seen the new season of their favorite TV show or listened to their favorite singer's new album. You can even discuss funny memes or tell them a funny story. Don't lose your positive attitude, and do try to remain upbeat.

If they keep going back to the same toxicity, you may not have a choice but to set boundaries or even cut them off.

Avoid Eye Contact

If you work with an energy vampire or tend to run into them in group situations, you should avoid making eye contact. Eye contact is usually an invitation to start a conversation which is the last thing you want to do with negative individuals.

Don't Take It Personally

As mentioned, negative people love criticizing, putting other people down, and blaming others for their misfortunes. Don't take anything they say personally. Whether they criticize you or belittle your accomplishments, understand that this has nothing to do with you. This is about them and their inadequacies. When you don't take anything they say personally, you take their power from them. You need to understand that nothing they say or do has anything to do with you.

Understand This Isn't Your Energy

If you are constantly surrounded by toxic energy, you may think that this is your vibe or that there is something wrong with you. This is a big problem for HSP and empaths since they absorb other people's emotions, so it is sometimes hard to distinguish their feelings from someone else's. For this reason, you should separate yourself from negative energies and understand that they aren't your own. Seeing this distinction will protect you from letting other people's negativity consume you. This is usually done by practicing self-care, which will be discussed in detail in the next chapters.

Building Strong Relationships

Now that you understand what toxic energy is, how you can identify it, and protect yourself from it, you need to focus on building relationships with positive and healthy people. To preserve your energy and protect your well-being, you should make mindful decisions about who you spend your time with. Whether it is family, friends, co-workers, or romantic partners, be picky with the people you give your time to. According to various studies, the more time we spend with someone, the more we become like them. According to motivational speaker Jim Rohn "*We are the average of the five people we spend the most time with.*" So, take a good look at those closest to you. Are they the kind of people you want to be like? You want to try to be around people who build you up, celebrate your successes, support you, and make you feel better and energized after spending time with them.

"*Show me who your friends are, and I will tell you who you are*" is a famous saying that is pretty accurate. People rub off on each other, and, as an HSP, you should always surround yourself with mentally and emotionally healthy people so you only absorb positive energies. Many people don't realize the impact their relationships have on their mental health, psyche, and overall well-being. Therefore, focus on quality rather than quantity. Choose people who will push you to better yourself and your life. According to a 2013 study, people who lack self-control usually befriend people who are more self-disciplined so they can motivate them to increase their willpower and establish healthy habits. So be around people who motivate you to keep going and be the best version of yourself that you can be, rather than holding you back.

Even if you love a certain person or if they are family, keep loving them from a distance if they are toxic and harmful to your well-being. Be protective of your time and energy, and don't waste them on negative people. Don't jump into friendships or relationships so soon. Feel their energy and how you feel after spending time with them first. Do you feel drained or upbeat? You need to focus on what they say, how they act, how they talk about other people, how they treat you, how they treat animals, and how they listen to you. Simply put, pay attention to every little detail about them.

Take your time to get to know someone first before you decide if this relationship is worth investing your time in or not. Being aware of social vampire traits and identifying toxic energies will make it easy for you to determine who to let into your life and who to steer clear of. You need to build and maintain healthy and strong relationships with good people you can trust and who bring out the best in you. Like being surrounded by negative people can drain you, healthy relationships can be very beneficial.

How Healthy Relationships Affect Your Well-Being

We need to have people in our lives to connect with. It is human nature. In fact, many scientific studies have shown that social relationships can boost your health and make you live longer as they can protect you from cardiovascular diseases and high blood pressure and speed cancer recovery. Additionally, other studies have shown that having people in your life who love you, support you, and care about you can have a huge impact on your physical and mental health. Healthy relationships also reduce stress and give you a sense of purpose.

Better Lifestyle

When you are around happy people who lead a healthy lifestyle, you acquire healthy habits. People who better themselves and their lives will influence you to do the same. Friends or partners who work out and eat healthily will push you to work on yourself and make better choices to improve your lifestyle as well.

Reduce Stress

Having people in your life who love you, support you, and provide you with positivity will reduce your stress. Knowing someone has your back will make you feel safe, less alone, and change your whole outlook on life.

Speed Your Healing

According to research, heart surgery patients who have supportive partners do feel less anxious about surgery and can tolerate post-surgery pain. Having supportive relationships in your life will push you to beat pain and diseases because you know you aren't alone, and you have people in your life who can't wait to see you back on your feet.

Help You Grow

Unlike energy vampires who rain on your parade, having healthy relationships encourages you to chase after your dreams. They celebrate all your successes, no matter how small, giving you the motivation to keep going. They believe in you, which, in turn, boosts your confidence and makes you believe in yourself as well. You'll take risks and grow whether in your career, studies, or life in general because you have a strong support system rooting for you.

Even if you fail, you know they will be there for you to help you back on your feet so you can keep going.

Make building healthy relationships a priority for the sake of your mental, physical, and emotional health. You should also maintain these relationships and strengthen them. As an empath, this will come easy to you since you, more than anyone else, understand other people's emotions and make them feel seen and heard with no judgment. You'll also be sympathetic and understanding to their needs. Once you find a good friend and partner, work on increasing your bond and protecting your relationship with them. Good friends are hard to find.

Affirmations for Healthy and Loving Relationships

To build and maintain healthy and loving relationships, you should keep reminding yourself to strengthen these relationships every day. Finding the right words will inspire you to love yourself and the people in your life more.

- I love my (friends, family, and partner) more and more each day
- The people in my life support me to be better
- I trust the people in my life, and I can share all my secrets with them
- I am responsible for my own happiness
- I deserve love
- I am surrounded by love
- There is only space in my life for supportive people who want to see me grow
- I deserve to be happy
- I am grateful for all the people in my life
- I am responsible for how I feel
- I will create healthy boundaries
- I will respect other people's boundaries
- I will always choose kindness
- Healthy communication is key
- It is okay not to be right all the time

Checklist of Strategies to Identify Toxic Energies

Now that we reach the end of this chapter, we want to leave you with a checklist of strategies to help you identify toxic energies and how to block them out.

- You feel emotionally drained or exhausted after spending time with certain people
- You feel down after talking with them
- You always think of ways to get out of meeting them
- You avoid them or try to limit your interactions with them, even if you don't understand why
- You dread spending time with them, talking to them on the phone, or simply having a short interaction with them
- You feel you need time to recharge after spending time with them because they drain your energy
- You feel you need to speak to a friend after the bad day you had with the energy vampire
- Your ego may get the best of you, and you start stooping to their level, whether by using backhanded compliments or negative criticism
- You develop unhealthy habits to deal with the negativity like excessive eating or drinking
- You feel stressed and irritated and may even lose your temper after being around them for a long period of time
- Deep down, you know you aren't comfortable around them and that their vibe isn't right

To block these toxic energies out, you need to:

- Set healthy boundaries
- Keep your distance from them
- Avoid getting sucked into their drama
- Choose positivity
- Practice self-care
- Put yourself first and learn to say "No."

Empaths and HSP should always be on the lookout for toxic energy since it can damage your well-being. Pay attention to all the negative traits we have mentioned here and do your best to limit your interactions with these people. Remember, you are an empath if you feel uncomfortable around someone, but you can't put your finger on why you may be picking up on their toxic vibes. Trust your gut feeling when something doesn't feel right and either walk away or set boundaries.

Chapter 5: What Are Psychic Vampires?

Psychic vampires are individuals who drain the energy of others. They are named "vampires" because they either suck a person's auratic life force or deplete another person's emotions without reciprocating the same level of care and empathy. Everyone has unintentionally drained another person's energy at some point in life. The difference here is that even though energy vampires are not essentially aware that they're hurting those around them either, they do it constantly.

Interactions with psychic vampires are never healthy. They always receive far more energy than they give out in any social exchange. Having read the previous chapter, you can already tell how toxic these individuals can be. Spending a few minutes with them can leave you emotionally drained and exhausted.

This chapter will encounter telltale signs that a person is an energy vampire. You'll find out how they operate and conduct their attacks. The chapter also covers the different types of energy vampires and provides some tips on how to deal with each so you can protect your psyche.

Highly Sensitive People and Psychic Vampires

As an HSP, you need to understand why you're particularly at risk of being hurt by an energy vampire. Besides the fact that your high sensitivity makes you more vulnerable to their actions, psychic vampires are more likely to target you out of a group of people.

Since they are "vampires," they constantly need someone to feed off, and there is no better target than a kind-hearted, compassionate person. Being sensitive to the emotions and feelings of others puts you at a great advantage. However, it also makes you more likely to please others and do anything to accommodate them at the expense of your own well-being. Your high sensitivity allows you to sense when someone is in need, and unfortunately, energy vampires are great at playing the part. You are someone who listens and is willing to offer help without expecting anything in return, which is exactly what they need.

You make the perfect prey since you offer your energy without expecting the other person to reciprocate it, and they are not willing to offer their energy back.

How to Spot an Energy Vampire

The first and most vital step in dealing with energy vampires is learning how to identify them. You don't want to risk becoming attached to that person or investing a great deal of time, energy, and care in your relationship before realizing their toxic nature.

There are several types of energy vampires to look out for, which is something that we'll cover in more depth throughout this chapter. However, we believe it helps to gather a general insight into their characteristics and how they operate first.

Telltale Signs Someone Is an Energy Vampire

- Psychic vampires tend to be highly negative individuals. They always anticipate the worst and have a way of pointing out the negative aspects of every situation (yes, even positive ones).

- They are overly critical. They thrive off criticizing others and making fun of them. This is usually due to their own lack of self-esteem.

- Energy vampires seldom take responsibility for their actions. They will never hold themselves accountable for anything.

- It seems like they can never stop complaining. They always find something to sulk about, whether it's a certain situation or another person's actions and behaviors.

- They always play the victim and act like martyrs. They make it look like everyone is out to get them.
- You'll always find them entangled in any type of drama in the workplace, with friends, etc.
- Energy vampires try to bash others to show that they're better than them. They one-up them and do everything to prove that they're the most successful.
- They need to be the center of attention. Psychic vampires make everything about themselves and like to be the focal point of outings, events, meetings, parties, etc.
- They are manipulators. They know how to intimidate others and guilt trip them into getting everything they want.

When you're dealing with an energy vampire, they'll likely interrupt you whenever they get the chance to. They are the talkers in any conversation and never take the time to listen to others. Psychic vampires are usually the ones who spread gossip in the workplace or among friends. When you're finally finished interacting with them, you feel demotivated, down, "off," and completely out of energy.

Characteristics of an Energy Vampire

If you get to know an energy vampire on a personal level, you'll likely notice that they possess these personality traits:

- Energy vampires usually feel abandoned and rejected. This is perhaps why they always play the victim.
- They need validation and constant reassurance, which is a sign of low self-esteem. They may try to make themselves feel better by criticizing others, one-upping them, and being the center of attention.
- They are never satisfied. Psychic vampires struggle with a lack of feelings of fulfillment, which is why they complain so much.
- They need nurturing. A psychic vampire's behavior is usually a result of psychological issues and an unstable childhood. They may not have received adequate amounts of care, so they feed off highly sensitive and caring individuals.
- They are often tired and out of energy. Their negativity causes them to vibrate at a low energy level.

How They Operate

When a psychic vampire attacks its target, they experience a boost in energy levels. Meanwhile, their victim is left feeling exhausted and tired. People who thrive off another individual's energy do it unintentionally. The attack often happens when the energy vampire experiences a lack of energy and is therefore looking to recharge it.

Most psychic vampires have mental, physical, or emotional problems to deal with. They may struggle with feeling inadequate or insufficient, so they turn to feeding off other people to replenish their life force. It's important to note that these individuals are not necessarily bad people. Even though they are toxic to those around them, they're not consciously aware of their actions or how they affect others. That said, you still need to protect your energy. You are not responsible for helping them "fix" their condition, especially since no one can be helped if they don't want to help themselves. Additionally, the whole point behind this book is to help you, as an HSP, to prioritize your own needs and learn how to eliminate toxic energies from your lives.

So, how do you recognize a psychic attack?

First and foremost, your aura will feel disturbed and diminished. Besides experiencing significant energy loss and persistent fatigue, you may also experience sleep disturbances and mental confusion. Psychic attacks often accompany many physical ailments and illnesses, including headaches, muscle tension, and dizziness. When interacting with a psychic vampire, you'll likely feel irritable and experience a huge slump in your mood.

Dealing with Energy Vampires

It's not always feasible to cut contact with an energy vampire, especially when they're your co-worker, boss, or if you have to see them often. However, there are some things you can do to protect yourself and control where you direct your time and energy.

Becoming aware of the people who suck your life force will allow you to be mindful of your interactions with them. You can also carry protective stones and use the power of visualization to envision a shield or an auratic bubble that protects your energy whenever you're around them. Self-care and protection techniques and tools that can help you maintain and redeem your energy are widely expanded upon in the following chapters.

Here are some tips you can follow when interacting with an energy vampire:

- **Breathe deeply, and don't sweat it.** Don't let their words influence you and take up headspace. As an HSP, it's easy to take things to heart. However, you have to remind yourself that their behavior is not personal.

- Being highly sensitive also comes with the tendency to find excuses for other people's actions. You need to remind yourself that **their behaviors and words are never acceptable.** Giving them excuses enables their actions and permits them.

- As we mentioned in the previous chapter, change the focus when you're discussing heavier subjects. It's always best if you keep the conversations light. When they say something you don't like, try not to react.

- Remind yourself of the nature of your relationship. Are you friends? Co-workers? How easily can you walk away?

- Take a moment to put things into perspective. It's easy to let their words affect you. But before you do so, are their words and actions a reflection of them or you?

- **Know your value and worth.** Why would you allow an energy vampire to suck the life out of you when you can hang out with people who appreciate your caring and compassionate nature?

Understanding Energy Vampires

Energy vampires are everywhere. They can ruin our lives and hurt us if we're not careful around them. But why is that? Trauma is the answer. People who hurt others, intentionally or not, are usually brought up in unstable environments. There are other psychological reasons why someone may deplete the energy of those around them. However, this one is the most common.

The degree of instability or "vampirism" that they exhibit in their adulthood largely depends on the quality of their childhood. The higher the level of trauma they've experienced, the more intensely they'll express these behaviors. Most psychic vampires are the way they are because they had parents who behaved the same way.

Since they are likely to have been exposed to emotional vampirism long before they had a chance to develop their conscious minds, they may not realize the trauma they've experienced. Even though the individual doesn't grasp it, their subconscious mind does. This is why they inflict what they've learned or experienced on those around them. This cycle only breaks when their conscious mind comes to terms with what's happening.

Another common reason why energy vampires behave that way is that they're depleted themselves. We are all often exhausted, and there are always times when we feel completely out of balance. For some people, consuming the energy of others is a natural response. This sudden surge of life force can even become addictive.

Types of Energy Vampires

Energy vampires can be generally broken down into types. We are here to help you understand the difference between the three most common types of energy vampires and teach you how to deal with each one.

The Melodramatic Vampire

This type of energy vampire lacks any understanding of personal boundaries. They can't really tell the difference between things that can be appropriately shared with others and aren't aware of the limitations of their relationships with others. For instance, those individuals may share deeply personal information with their co-workers at work. Melodramatic vampires usually waste plenty of other people's time. They're very talkative and often like to believe that your relationship with them is much stronger than you think it is. They are often very wary and anxious about getting rejected. This is to the point where they can't detach from certain people or get over particular relationships when they need to. It becomes hard for anyone to peacefully remove themselves.

So, what can you do? Clear and direct communication is key to dealing with these people. You need to be to the point yet kind when dealing with them. When they touch on certain topics that you aren't comfortable discussing, make sure to let them know. You can also use your body language to communicate. For example, you can get up and start walking away to signal the end of a conversation.

The Egotistic Vampire

Like the melodramatic vampire, egotistic individuals take up much of your time. However, they do so because they believe they're entitled to it.

They think that whatever they have to say is more important than what anyone else wants to discuss. These individuals typically brag about their successes and accomplishments. They also tend to "one-up" others, bring them down, and downplay their achievements. Egotistic energy vampires always try to prove that they're better than others. When you try to oppose them or stand up to their ways, they will claim that you're highly sensitive and dramatic.

To deal with them, you need to understand that this type of behavior reflects a gap in having their needs met. Those individuals usually struggle to recognize their self-value and worth. While it isn't an ideal tactic, this is the only way in which they can feel important. Understanding this allows you to set appropriate boundaries with this individual. They don't care about your relationship as much as they care about the validation they receive from it. The trick here is to find a middle ground. While asserting yourself, give them something that fulfills their need for validation. For example, if you're dealing with this person at work, you can say something like, "I believe this is a great solution. However, considering our current resources, I think exploring (a different option) would be smart."

The Dependent Vampire

Dependent psychic vampires are in constant need of reassurance and assistance. They always refer to others for complete guidance on how to get things done. They may come off as people-pleasers because they never want to disappoint others. They are also worried that taking any unapproved actions will hinder your relationship or the general status quo. Giving in to their need for instruction and aid makes them more and more helpless. You may find it very hard to tell those types of people off, especially since their behavior is well-intentioned. They are afraid of letting you down, after all. However, their demand for nourishment can be very time-consuming and energetically draining.

The more you answer them and try to help them, the worse it will become. Instead of leaving you alone, they will always come to you whenever they need help or reassurance. They need someone to tell them that they're on the right track. When interacting with them, you should encourage them to find their own solutions to the problems. Be kind and give them positive feedback but don't try to fix things for them. Their dependency can be frustrating at times. Try to maintain your cool because responding impulsively or showing agitation can worsen things.

How to Reassess Your Relationships

Relationships are built on interactions and exchanges. You exchange words, actions, feelings, thoughts, and energies. Dealing with others can go one of both ways. They can make us feel happier or uplifted – or hinder our mood. This is why we need to be very careful when we deal with those around us. Maintaining our emotional, mental, physical, and spiritual health should be the top priority. We have to reassess our relationships and determine which individuals are worth keeping in our lives.

Here are some things you need to consider when re-evaluating your relationship with any person:

- Think back to the start of your relationship. Was it different from how it currently is? If so, are things better or worse than they were before?

- How much can you trust this person? Is this level of trust appropriate for the nature of your relationship? For instance, when it comes to friends and family, you should be able to trust them with your secrets, fears, etc. If you're reassessing your relationship with a co-worker, determine if you can trust them with confidential matters, and so on.

- Does the relationship make you feel valued, respected, loved, and supported? Again, you need to account for the nature of the relationship.

- Are your time and effort reciprocated or one-sided?

- Can you be yourself around this person, or do you often worry about them criticizing and judging you?

If you can tell for sure that someone is draining your energy, take the time to think about whether your relationship can change for the better. This will help you determine whether you need to let this person go or set new limits and boundaries.

Psychic vampires are everywhere. You are likely to come across at least one energy vampire in your life. Whether they're friends, bosses, family members, clients, or co-workers, you need to find an effective way to manage your relationship with them and deal with them. Otherwise, you'll feel uncomfortable, anxious, and frustrated whenever they're around. Psychic vampires can even diminish your self-confidence and esteem by making you doubt your own decisions, actions, and capabilities. Learning the telltale signs and understanding how they operate can help you protect your energy and set much-needed boundaries.

Chapter 6: Psychic Self-Defense

Now that you know how to identify toxic energies, it is time for you to learn how to defend against them. This chapter discusses psychic self-defense and how HSPs can use it to live happier and healthier lives. The basis of self-defense is mindfulness, which allows you to develop your intuition, empowering you to employ a protective energy shield whenever needed. You'll learn to recognize situations where your energy may be in danger of getting drained or tainted by someone else's issues. In addition, you'll develop a deeper appreciation toward yourself and others without feeling the need to get involved in their problems.

What Is Psychic Self Defense?

Generally speaking, self-defense is defined as an act of protecting oneself from being harmed by another person's influence on your psyche. Self-defense can be physical, but in this case, it's the defense of your mental health. For an HSP, practicing psychic self-defense can mean the difference between living a fulfilled life or hiding away as your energy gets drained by others. As you have learned in the previous chapter, psychic vampires can lurk in every corner. This makes the regular application of self-defense tactics even more crucial. However, this doesn't mean you have to view these tactics as a necessary evil. You don't have to live in fear of running into someone who will drain your energy or look for them so you can fight them off. You just have to learn how to deflect their attempts when you encounter them. So, in essence, psychic self-defense is a practice that lets you hone your defensive skills, so you can draw upon them when needed.

Mindfulness as Self-Defense

Essentially, psychic self-defense is a powerful term for mindfulness – which is what the protection against toxic energies should be based on. Mindfulness pays attention to our present exterior experiences with openness, curiosity, and willingness to be what is. During this practice, your mind is forced to remain focused, quiet, alert, and in the present. Any judgment or interpretation that may occur during a session must be acknowledged, then dismissed.

You can use mindfulness as a form of self-defense.
https://unsplash.com/photos/ie8WW5KUx3o

The main reason it's recommended for these purposes is that it's very effective in preventing others from corrupting your energy. When you are focused, you learn to keep only thoughts about the present in the forefront of your mind. You aren't letting yourself get distracted by any other ideas or opinions, which is most likely how your energy gets drained.

Achieving mindfulness will allow you to maintain a high level of energy and use it for your needs without risking it getting drained. Practicing mindfulness can prepare you for an encounter with a psychic vampire – which happens more often than you think. We have all encountered situations like this before, where our energy was drained before we even knew it.

The Benefits of Mindfulness for HSP

One of the most common struggles of an HSP is overthinking their actions. You are constantly worrying about whether you are doing something right and require frequent affirmations on why you are doing it in the first place. Fortunately, practicing mindfulness doesn't mean you have to fixate on all the advantages of your technique, no matter how gratifying they may be. And you don't even have to focus your energy on learning any new skills. You just have to work on what you already know and possess. This familiarity puts HSPs at ease, which is another plus as you may find changes overwhelming. Whether you have practiced mindfulness before or not, you have an innate ability to live in the present. You just have to learn how to cultivate it to gain the most out of it.

You won't need to learn something new, but you also won't need to change who you are either. While you may need to make a few adjustments to your schedule and lifestyle at the beginning of your journey, you won't have to go as far as turning into someone else. It probably wouldn't work either - as you are often reluctant to let go of familiar things. Mindfulness cultivates who you are on the inside, allowing you to express your wants and needs during a session.

Apart from gaining insight, practicing mindfulness also results in reduced anxiety levels, enhanced performance, and experiencing the world around you with new eyes. This, in turn, empowers you with kindness, compassion, and love toward yourself and others. It may also teach you to become more curious and hone your toxic energy detecting skills. This benefits you, your loved ones, your work colleagues, and your neighbors - and, depending on how active you are in your community - it will affect a lot more people.

Another thing you may struggle with as an HSP is self-care. Mindfulness can transform your mind into a "My needs don't matter as much as other people's needs" mentality into an "I am acknowledging my needs and should work on fulfilling them" mindset. And the best thing about using mindfulness is that it's independent of belief systems. It's a way of living that can be incorporated into anyone's schedule, making sure it meets their needs.

Since you probably do everything to avoid conflict, you'll be glad to know that mindfulness effectively reduces all the stress these situations cause you. This innovative approach is a much-needed guide in this complex and uncertain world filled with wants and needs. It teaches you an effective solution even for issues you thought to be beyond repair.

It is worth mentioning that there is a common misconception that mindfulness is only about using your mental energy to resolve issues. This often causes people to try to force their thoughts in a certain direction, worrying only about whether what they are doing in their heads is good enough. When, in fact, it's your body that allows you to go into the practice in the first place. Without your lungs, you won't be able to take calming breaths, which is often an introductory exercise to mindfulness techniques. Negative energy affects your body just as badly as it does with your mind and spirit – and sometimes even more. After all, your energy is also susceptible to gravity, making it travel downward from your head to the rest of your body, bringing all the negativity with it. Becoming aware of all the sensations in your body is the second part of the self-care you need to work on.

Intuition and Mindfulness

Intuition is the knowledge that comes to you without taking any conscious steps to invoke it. The subconscious part of your mind generates it as it sifts through past experiences. As your brain drifts away from your experiences, it also notes what you have learned from them. So, when you are at a loss on how to proceed with a similar situation, it automatically guides you through the new experience. And, yet again, it processes and registers how things happened without your brain's conscious awareness.

Intuition is also called a gut feeling because it comes from deep within. It shows you the best way to go, even if you can't see it that way – which is why you often ignore it. This is where mindfulness practices come in handy. They encourage you to tap into your subconscious and listen to whatever it tells you. Intuition is a unique approach to considering your thoughts, feelings, and actions.

Consequently, not everyone relies on their intuition regularly. Some can accept whatever their gut tells them as an absolute fact, while others prefer deliberate reflection. In addition, the aforementioned ability to store information about past experiences also varies in different people. The brains of some individuals can file away a lot more complex information than others. Some just have a very narrow scope of experience to learn from, so when they start facing new experiences, their brain doesn't have any references to compare them to.

Fortunately, an HSP doesn't have any trouble processing things thoroughly because their brain hones in on every little detail possible. This is a considerable strength - which you absolutely must take advantage of when learning psychic self-defense. Listening to your inner voice makes much more sense because your subconscious mind has a much more extensive database to work with. However, being sensitive to other people's feelings can make you lose touch with this intuitive guide. Either you don't even notice it's there or ignore it completely, regardless of how many similar experiences you have had. Being influenced by someone else's energy (or being drained from your own) often leads to confusion. You may end up thinking others know better or that you have to agree with them to maintain your relationships. It's all useless anyway because no matter how hard you try, you'll never be able to please everyone.

As an HSP, listening to one's intuition is incredibly beneficial, and not only because it tells you what to do. Listening to its message is fundamental for many reasons. Intuition, in fact, acts as an emotional anchor, allowing you to sort through all your feelings and impulses and find what's not yours. You may also see that the solution you are trying to apply to an issue you thought was yours doesn't work because you just took over someone else's issues. And because your mind is in constant chatter even without another person's problems to deal with. A mindfulness practice aimed at awakening your intuition will bring you peace and happiness.

But how can HSPs take advantage of intuition? The answer to that is fairly simple. You are constantly interacting with your environment, including with people who you live or work with. More often than not, you need to change the direction in which your relationship is developing. And your inner voice unveils which path you should follow. As you can see, when fully developed, intuition can be an effective tool. But for this to happen, you'll need to practice mindfulness daily.

Several links tie mindfulness to intuition, and here are some of the most important ones:

- **Being Present:** As mentioned before, the core of every mindfulness exercise is centering your mind on the present time. Whether you are haunted by negative experiences in your past or are dreading a future event, your mind is bombarded by a sea of distracting thoughts you can't control. These thoughts and feelings cause the stress that comes with the blocking out of your intuition. By becoming mindful and grounding yourself in the present, you protect your intuition.

- **Understanding Yourself:** Learning how to recognize your gut feeling is not easy. You don't know yourself well enough to predict whether you can stay away from an energy vampire or not. Mindfulness allows you to explore the deepest corners of yourself and develop positive feelings toward them. As you get to know your values, you start to appreciate them, and, as a consequence, they empower you with self-love, kindness, and much more. Understanding where your values lie enables your gut to guide you toward paths that are aligned with those values.

- **Learning to Trust Yourself:** After spending so much time subjected to the energy of others, you simply cannot trust yourself not to fall under their spell again. The good thing about developing your intuition is that you know it comes from a trusted source. Even though it relies on using your intuition instead of your mind, your mind knows that you have already made those choices before (and they were the right ones), so you can trust them once again.

All these benefits can be achieved throughout the mindfulness journey. But you must be prepared to listen very closely to recognize that inner voice. This may take some time to achieve, so don't be discouraged if it doesn't happen right away. Just as with other skills, the power of intuition can be honed, and it should often be. The intrinsic knowledge your mind filed away only takes you so far on your journey. Your mind often needs feedback to compare an experience with the present one. Being an HSP does have advantages in that area, but it doesn't guarantee you'll be successful without training your mind to respond correctly to an energetic crisis.

Using an Energy Shield

Another reason to practice mindfulness is that it teaches you how to use an energy shield. Even though not inviting a person with toxic energy into your space is a sure way to avoid becoming drained, this isn't always an option. After all, you can just cease contact with a close relative who relies on your assistance or who you have a tight emotional bond with. Nor can you leave a workplace without having another option lined up already, simply because one of your colleagues is an energy vampire. So, the best way to defend yourself from the psychic vampires in your life is by putting up a guard to protect yourself. Remember, these are people who drain vital energy to substitute their own. However, they often do it without even being aware of it, so confronting them is not a viable solution. Their energy may be tainted by the negativity they carry due to mental or physical issues. As an HSP, you are very susceptible to these energies, and you may find yourself adopting them without even realizing it. The other person's inability to deal with their issues becomes your problem, and you don't even understand what's happening. Becoming aware of their toxic energy is the first step toward understanding how to shield yourself.

The second solution is to learn how to put up a barrier, so the effects of their attack may be less damaging. Practicing mindfulness can help you develop this shield by channeling your energy into visualizing it or sensing it in another way. There are many ways to bring up this protective layer between you and the toxic energy source. Visualizing your shield as a colored field of light around you is one of the most widely used options. It relies on the theory that different colors vibrate on a different frequency, so whatever frequency you vibrate on at a particular time is represented in the color of your energetic shield. While this may sound like a simple task, you may find it quite challenging if you aren't familiar with mindfulness techniques. Unlike any other defense method that may tap into energy from outside the body, this one relies on using your willpower and doing what feels right for you. To put it simply, you must go with your gut – which takes us back to the role of mindfulness in developing intuition. This indicates that all these factors are interconnected: mindfulness, gut feelings, and protective shields. Although practicing mindfulness is considered a stepping stone to developing the other two, doing so will make you better in this practice. Having a strong intuition will help you use the protection more effectively.

It may tell you how and when to pull out a shield and how large it should be. Sometimes, a person's tainted energy affects the energy of the objects around them. If you, as an HSP, spend long hours surrounded by the same environment they are in, you may risk having your energy drained even through objects. In this case, your shield must extend to those items, as well, to keep yourself safe.

Remember that shields can lose their powers, especially if you find yourself in a stressful situation you haven't encountered before. This may cause your energy to be depleted, causing your protection to wear off after only 2-3 hours. However, in a relaxed environment, the shield will probably stay strong for the length of an average workday. So, it's a good idea to re-establish it from time to time – once again using your go-to mindfulness exercises. This is also a good way to practice calming yourself in a stressful environment, which, for an HSP, can be even more difficult to bear.

Final Thoughts

Psychic self-defense is about protecting yourself from toxic energy around you. It uses mindfulness, or an open state of mind, in which you focus on channeling your thoughts and energy onto what's important to you rather than what someone else needs. It's best applied against psychic vampires – who you interact with regularly and who you can't avoid. Learning how to deal with these people is particularly challenging for an HSP as it requires a lot of will and self-discipline. Make sure you practice mindfulness regularly by taking enough time to develop the protection you need. Learning to listen to your gut when it may be a good idea to pull up an energy-protecting shield will also teach you the importance of being patient and working toward your goals.

Chapter 7: Self-Care and Setting Boundaries

We have discussed in previous chapters toxic energies and energy vampires. These people are all around us, whether they are family members, friends, co-workers, or even our partners. As mentioned, HSPs and empaths are more prone to be affected by toxic energies. For this reason, you need to practice self-care and set boundaries to protect yourself from negativity.

Unfortunately, many people don't practice self-care. They always claim that they don't have time for it. They are either busy with their career, studying, or taking care of their kids. There is a misconception that taking some time for yourself is selfish or a luxury that not everyone can afford. You need to understand that self-care isn't about doing something extravagant like taking a few days off and flying to Paris (however, if you can afford it, go for it). It is about doing what makes you happy and relaxed, even if it is binge-watching the new season of your favorite TV show. Simply put, do what you enjoy, what puts a smile on your face, and what makes you feel good. Self-care is different for every individual, so what works for others may not work for you.

Self-care is a necessity, not an indulgence. When you take care of yourself, your physical, mental, and emotional health improve, and other aspects of your life flourish as well. It is vital for everyone, especially for HSPs. Being exposed to toxic energies is draining, so you need to take some time every day to recharge and give your brain some time to relax.

Spending the whole day absorbing everyone's energies and dealing with negativity is exhausting. It can affect your health, sleep pattern, and cause various mental health issues like anxiety and depression. Assigning some time each day for self-care will do wonders for your mental health. Self-care practices include exercising, meditation, eating healthy, sleeping well, and having strong and healthy relationships. It is about having healthy habits, a healthy lifestyle, and being surrounded by positive people.

As an empath, protecting your energy should be your number one priority. If you don't guard your energy, the vampires in your life will keep "sucking" it until nothing is left. You'll be burned out and too tired to do anything, and all aspects of your life will suffer as a result. However, this doesn't have to happen every time you are around negative people. Practicing self-care will protect you from feeling drained. You'll start to feel energetic and focused; your mood will improve, you'll be able to think clearly, and you'll notice an improvement in all areas of your life.

You probably imagine taking a bath, meditating, or practicing yoga when you think of self-care. However, if you have toxic people in your life, setting boundaries is also considered self-care. Having healthy boundaries helps you protect your energy. They act like shields that keep out all the negativity and toxicity. Boundaries protect you from feeling drained and overwhelmed. It is easier for most people to distinguish between their energy and other people's. However, this can be impossible for an empath as they are walking sponges taking in everyone else's emotions. However, boundaries allow you to separate your energies and emotions from others.

They give you power against energy vampires. Due to your sensitive and empathetic nature, you may find it difficult to set boundaries. Naturally, you are afraid to hurt other people's feelings, so you would be reluctant to say no to them or cut them off. However, you shouldn't feel guilty for looking out for yourself. Energy vampires are toxic people, and, as mentioned before, you can't change or fix them. If you don't have boundaries, these people will keep taking and taking from you until there is nothing left.

You have probably had a friend or a family member tell you that you need to "set some boundaries." However, as a sensitive person who puts others' needs before their own, you may feel that having boundaries goes against your sensitive nature. You need to understand that this isn't selfish, rude, or cruel, it is very healthy, and most people do it. It gives you power and control over your life.

Understanding Boundaries

To understand the importance of boundaries, you first need to know what boundaries are. In simple terms, think of it as an imaginary line that you draw between yourself and others, and no one is allowed to cross it. You are basically setting rules about what you accept and what you don't. This helps you maintain your energy to feel comfortable in your relationships. Having healthy boundaries will protect you from the negative people in your life. You'll be able to say "no" to things you aren't comfortable with, like avoiding a family dinner because your toxic cousin who enjoys bringing everyone down will be there, or not answering the phone when your negative friend who never stops complaining calls.

According to the Canadian Mental Health Association, setting healthy boundaries will protect you from people who keep crossing the line with their demands and the control toxic individuals have over you. Several studies have shown that a lack of boundaries can make you resentful, less happy, and exhausted. However, a different study has shown that setting boundaries can improve your well-being and make you feel empowered. Healthy boundaries will boost your self-esteem, give you a sense of self and self-respect, and make others respect you.

You should set boundaries with your family, friends, partner, and co-workers. Boundaries aren't always about saying no or keeping people at a distance; this isn't healthy. Boundaries are communicating with the people in your life what you'll tolerate and what you won't and saying no to negativity. So, when a good friend asks you to help them move and have the time, you can say yes since this is something you are doing on your own terms. However, when someone toxic asks you to drop everything to drive them to the airport, saying no is how you set boundaries. Simply put, don't apply the same boundaries to everyone. Have different boundaries, and make sure to set strict ones for the negative people in your life.

Setting boundaries is for you and your well-being. Don't think of how other people will feel or react when choosing yourself first. You aren't selfish, as this is a form of self-care. Do you feel guilty when you meditate or work out? It is the same thing. You are taking care of yourself and protecting your energy from people who are harming your mental and emotional health.

Self-Care and Well-Being

Life isn't always easy. It is filled with stress and worry. You need to be strong mentally, emotionally, and physically to face whatever life throws at you. Our energy is what allows us to handle everything in life, the positive and the negative. Self-care can have a huge impact on your well-being because it lowers your stress levels, makes you more relaxed, and improves your emotional well-being. It also increases your self-esteem, improves your mood, and enriches your relationships. This will, in turn, have a huge impact on your physical health.

For instance, if you have to interact with a negative person at work, you'll go back home feeling exhausted and drained. You won't be able to do any chores or have the energy to sit and chat with your family. Surrendering to this feeling and doing nothing will make things worse, and eventually, you won't have the energy to get out of bed. On the other hand, self-care practices like meditation will help recharge your energy. Taking a few minutes each day to sit in a quiet spot and being mindful and aware of how you feel in this present moment will calm your brain and help you recharge. Meditation will also help reduce your stresses and allow you to focus on the here and now, which will boost your energy right back to 100%.

How to Incorporate Self-Care into Daily Activities

Now that you understand the importance of self-care to protect your energy and improve your well-being, you should learn how to incorporate it into your daily routine.

Choose the Right Self-Care Practice For You

If you decide to exercise every day and you hate physical activities, this will feel like a punishment instead of self-care. So, write down all the activities you enjoy that make you feel relaxed. Once you have an idea of what you want to do to unwind, you can incorporate it into your routine.

Wake Up Early

The way you start your day will set the tone for the rest of the day. You probably wake up, get dressed, and drive to work, and if you have kids, you cater to their needs first. However, we suggest that you wake up 30 minutes earlier every day to practice self-care. Whether you'll meditate, write in your journal, exercise, or practice yoga, you need some peace and quiet to take care of yourself without any distractions. So, make waking up early a habit and take a few minutes each morning to recharge and relax.

Set Realistic Goals

Setting realistic goals will protect you from feeling discouraged and motivate you to keep going. For instance, if you can't start exercising for an hour every day, you'll burn yourself out, which defies the whole purpose of self-care. Start small and increase the time incrementally.

Take Breaks

You don't have to wait until you get home to practice self-care. Instead of eating at the office, take advantage of your lunch break and go for a walk. This will boost your mood and make you feel refreshed.

Check on Yourself

Give yourself a month after incorporating self-care. Is what you are doing working? Do you feel better than when you started or the same? Do you feel energized after every practice? If the answer is "yes," then what you are doing is working, so keep going. However, if the answer is "no," you'll need to make a few changes, like opting for different practices.

Use Technology

Although technology, like social media, can play a huge role in draining your energy, it also has its advantages. You can use different apps to help you create a self-care routine, like a workout app with simple exercises to try at home, a guided meditation app, or an app to remind you to drink water. Whatever the self-care practice you choose, you'll most likely find an app for it.

How to Prioritize Self-Care as an HSP

Just like setting boundaries, self-care for HSP may not be so easy due to their nature. HSPs are easily overwhelmed not just by energies and emotions but by simple things like smells or sounds. You are also always worried since you feel everything deeply. Unlike most people, you'll need to work harder to calm your thoughts, relax, and restore your energy. As we have mentioned earlier, if you don't take care of yourself, your well-being will suffer.

For this reason, you should prioritize self-care. Think of your energy like your phone battery. If you don't recharge it every day, what will happen? Your phone will eventually die. You need to make a decision and incorporate self-care into your daily routine. Decide that you'll make yourself a priority, and don't let anything or anyone (especially the energy vampires in your life) discourage you.

You may be thinking, how can I prioritize self-care when I don't have enough time? Believe it or not, you have the time. You just don't regard self-care as something as essential as taking your kids to soccer practice or finishing your work before the deadline. Understand that you aren't just someone's parent or an employee in an office. Find your own identity, and figure out who you are. Who are you without a family to take care of or a job to go to? Once you see yourself as an individual who needs looking after, you'll sympathize with your own needs and begin to work on yourself. Understand that you aren't someone who plays a role in other people's stories; you are the star of your own and should be treated as such.

Treat yourself with the same kindness as you treat others with. Be sympathetic towards your own needs. Most importantly, you should know that, just like boundaries, there is nothing selfish about self-care. In fact, it may benefit the people in your life since it will give you the energy to take care of them as well. So, find the time for yourself and prioritize it just like you prioritize other things in your life.

Don't allow the energy vampires in your life to interfere with your downtime. For instance, your toxic friend may want you to help them move, but you are exhausted and need a break. They may guilt you into helping them, and, as an HSP, you may be unable to say "no" because you feel their needs come first. When you care about your well-being and understand how vital it is to take some time for yourself, it will be impossible for you to give it up for anything or anyone. However, what if your toxic friend keeps interfering with your self-care routine? Well, this is where setting healthy boundaries come in.

How to Set Boundaries as an HSP

Setting boundaries is one of the most important forms of self-care because it gives you power and control over your time and energy.

Identify Your Boundaries

You can't set boundaries without first identifying what they are. One of the main reasons you set boundaries is to protect your energy. So, you should first figure out which actions drain you and make you uncomfortable so you can set the appropriate boundaries. You should also determine what actions you'll tolerate and what actions you won't put up with.

Start Small

If this is your first time setting boundaries, you should start small, so you don't overwhelm yourself or feel guilty. For instance, if you have a toxic friend who constantly calls you to complain, try to limit your interactions with them. You don't have to say yes every time they ask you to meet. Next, don't answer their calls when you are exhausted or busy. Simply send them a message letting them know you don't feel like talking – and will call them back later. This will help you build the courage to set bigger boundaries and say "no" to anything that makes you uncomfortable.

Avoid Maybes

Sometimes, an HSP struggles with saying "no" to avoid confrontation and upsetting others. They just say "maybe" instead. When it comes to boundaries, there are no maybes or gray areas. You should be straightforward about what you want and what you don't want. The toxic people in your life will take advantage of your reluctance and turn "maybe" into "yes." Whatever you choose, make sure it is what you want.

Embrace Your Sensitivity

Embracing your sensitivity will make you more aware and accepting of your strengths and weaknesses. This way, you'll be able to set boundaries with these limitations in mind. For instance, if you find scary movies to be disturbing, say "no" when your friend suggests you watch one. Don't fight your nature just to please someone. It's the same with energy vampires. Understanding that these people have a negative impact on you due to your sensitivity will motivate you to set boundaries and stick to them.

Follow Your Gut Feeling

We have mentioned in a previous chapter that sometimes toxic energies are felt. A person doesn't have to do something specific. You just sense a vibe that makes you uncomfortable. In this case, don't wait for proof and follow your gut. Once you encounter someone that gives off bad vibes, immediately set boundaries.

No Is a Complete Sentence

No means no. Setting boundaries is being able to say "no" without having to explain yourself or being guilted into changing your mind. As an HSP, you may be reluctant to say "no" to avoid confrontation or hurting other people's feelings. However, you should never do something that you don't want, and don't be afraid to stand up for yourself. Most "normal" people in your life will understand and respect your choices. They won't be upset or make a big deal about it. However, the toxic ones will use guilt and anger when you refuse their demands, but you shouldn't give in and clarify that "No" is a complete sentence.

Cut People Off

In severe cases, you may have to cut the energy vampires off. If they don't respect your boundaries and are dangerous to your mental health, you should then prioritize your well-being and say bye-bye. You can try talking to them first but, as mentioned, you can't change people. So instead of remaining in a relationship or a friendship that keeps draining you, simply walk away. However, if this person is a close family member or a boss, you should try to limit your interactions with them as much as you can.

Self-Care Activities
Take a long bath
Go shopping
Drink your favorite cup of coffee in the morning and savor the taste
Practice yoga
Limit your time on social media
Avoid overwhelming places and toxic people
Do something fun (like playing video games or dancing)
Eat your favorite food
Spend time with your pet

Practice gratitude
Paint
Read
Travel
Spend time with positive and upbeat people
Have a good night's sleep
Be aware of your feelings throughout the day
Slow down and learn to live and enjoy the present moment
Set boundaries
Schedule time every day to practice your favorite hobby
Spend some time by yourself to recharge

Healthy Boundaries

- Say "no" if you don't want to do something
- Be firm when it comes to your boundaries
- Protect your personal space
- Communicate your boundaries
- Understand your limits
- Understand that you can't fix other people
- Don't accept blame for things that aren't your fault
- Set boundaries early in your relationships
- Limit your communication with toxic people

- Have physical boundaries (make it clear if you aren't big on hugs or you don't like to be touched)
- Create sexual boundaries (like asking your partner to use a condom or discuss what pleases you and what doesn't)
- Create material boundaries (you shouldn't say yes if you are uncomfortable with lending money or your car)
- Emotional boundaries (communicate your feelings and ensure they are being respected, like texting a friend when they call you and explaining you don't feel like talking now but will call later)
- Ensure your thoughts, ideas, and opinions are respected even if the other person doesn't agree with them
- Be protective of your time (you don't have to say yes to every invitation or answer every phone call if you don't feel like it)
- Walk away when your boundaries aren't respected

Remember to always be firm but kind when setting boundaries and can distinguish between energy vampires and your good friends or family members who are simply calling to say "Hi" or who need a favor.

Chapter 8: Toolbox for Protecting Your Energy

This chapter will talk about the different tools you can use to protect your energy. Just like some activities and techniques can protect you from negativity, some tools do the same job. Although energy can't be seen, certain tools are known to purify and cleanse negative energy so that positive vibes only surround you. Some of these tools include:

- Essential oils that you can use for massages or as ingredients in bath bombs. These oils are known to promote relaxation and improve your mood

- Crystals that you can place around your house, carry in your pocket or purse, or wear around your neck

- Adding salt to your bath water

- Burning dry sage

- Ringing handheld bells around the house

- Foods like lemon, cinnamon, and turmeric can absorb negative energy

Essential oils are great for relaxation.
https://unsplash.com/photos/jbjmimlaC-U

Activities to Implement in Your Daily Routine

In the previous chapter, we gave you an idea of how to incorporate self-care into your daily routine. Now, we will talk about some of the activities you can practice every day to protect yourself as an HSP from negative energies.

Meditation

Meditation is a practice where you sit in a relaxing position in a quiet spot, remain still, and only focus on your breathing. The purpose of meditation is to keep you focused and aware of the present moment, and it has a huge impact on your mental and emotional well-being.

Meditation also protects your energy and prevents negativity from getting to you. It should be incorporated into your daily routine until it becomes a habit, and the best way to achieve that is by assigning time for it every day. You'll only need 10 or 20 minutes, so make it a habit to wake up 20 minutes early. Stick to morning meditation as this is the only free time you may have all day. Most people are busy with work or kids throughout the day. You may be busy or too exhausted in the evenings and just want to go to bed.

If mornings aren't an option, schedule any time during the day. Just make sure that you stick to it. If this is your first time practicing mediation, you can start small. Practice for 5 minutes, then increase the time as you feel comfortable with it. You can also use apps that can guide you through your meditation and remind you every day to practice.

Exercise

Exercise helps protect your energy.
Creative Commons Zero (CC0) license *https://www.pexels.com/photo/woman-with-white-sunvisor-running-40751*

Another activity that will help protect your energy is exercise. Like meditation, start small, especially if you aren't an active person. Start with simple exercises like yoga, dancing, or going for walks. You must choose something you enjoy to keep doing it every day. Don't burn yourself out by opting for heavy exercises or exercising for long periods of time at first. You can begin with 15 or 20 minutes each day and go up from there. It will also help you if you can find a friend to exercise with so you can motivate each other. Try listening to music or exercising in a nice environment to make the experience more enjoyable.

Add exercise to your daily routine by scheduling time for it and sticking to it.

Take Long Walks in Nature

Being near nature is a sure way to make you feel recharged and relaxed. You must spend time outdoors every day. However, going to work and getting stuck in traffic doesn't count. You should be out in nature to enjoy some peace and quiet. Wake up 30 minutes early every day and take a walk in any green space near you, like a park, a forest, or your garden.

If you want to practice all these activities, we suggest you exercise or go for walks before meditation. It is best to meditate after physical activities to reap all the benefits.

Tools to Protect and Nurture Your Body

When you take care of your physical body, your mental and emotional health will thrive as a result. The following tools will have a huge impact on your physical health.

Hydration

No one can deny the importance of drinking enough water. Water is beneficial to your body, organs, and skin. According to Dr. Lindsay Baker, a scientist at the Gatorade Sports Science Institute, you can be hydrated when you drink other fluids like juice, coffee, or tea and eat water-based fruits and vegetables. However, the healthiest and best option is always water.

Water will make you feel energized, prevent migraines caused by dehydration, improve digestion, detoxify the body from harmful substances, improve heart health, and helps you to lose or manage your weight. It increases metabolism and reduces hunger. It also prevents kidney stones, reduces joint pain, prevents heat stroke, and helps regulate your body's temperature. According to a 2015 study, drinking enough water every day plays a huge role in improving your skin's health. Another study that took place in the same year showed that dehydration could cause constipation in elderly citizens.

A study that took place in 2011 proved that not drinking enough water can affect your concentration and mood. Therefore, make sure that you drink over 2 liters of water per day if you are a female and over 3 liters if you are male. However, you can drink more during hot weather if you are more active or if you suffer from a disease that causes symptoms that can leave you dehydrated.

Clean Food

You have probably been told before to watch what you eat. Many of us lead busy lives, so we don't have time to prepare healthy meals, and we end up eating junk food and unhealthy meals instead. However, junk food doesn't have any of the nutrients your body needs. You can treat yourself every once in a while to your favorite pizza or hotdog sandwich but focus on eating clean food regularly. Clean food includes all healthy foods like fruit, vegetables, dairy, protein, and grains. They contain all the minerals, healthy fats, and vitamins your body needs to boost your energy, improve your immunity, and prevent weight gain.

According to a study published in the American Journal of Epidemiology, eating whole grains every day can help you live longer as it decreases the mortality rate by 10%. A 2015 study showed that consuming fish, fruit, and vegetables can improve your memory. Additionally, eating clean food makes your nails stronger and your skin glow.

Sage

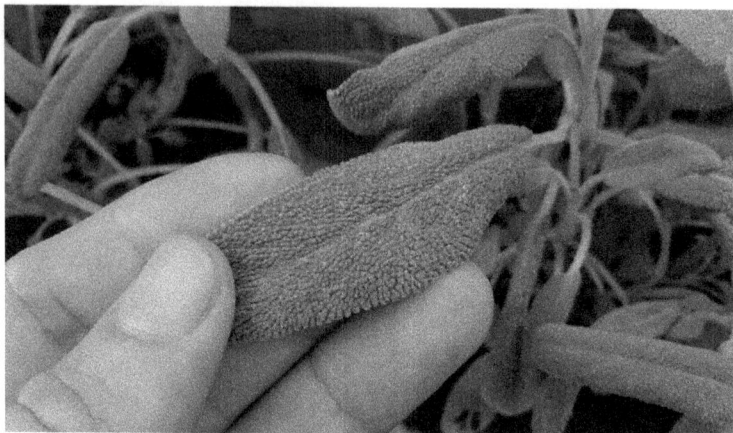

Sage.

Mokkie, CC BY-SA 3.0 https://creativecommons.org/licenses/by-sa/3.0 , via Wikimedia Commons: https://commons.wikimedia.org/wiki/File:Sage_(Salvia_officinalis).jpg

Sage is an herb that belongs to the mint family. Its leaves are gray-green and oval. It is very popular due to its earthy flavor and strong scent, and it is incorporated in various recipes. You can buy it either fresh or dried. In addition to its benefits in protecting your energy, sage can be very beneficial to your health as well.

Sage contains vitamin K, which promotes bone health. It also contains antioxidants that can improve your memory, reduce the risk of cancer, and can be a great treatment for diarrhea. According to a recent study, sage can improve your cognitive skills. Another study showed that sage can lower glucose levels in the blood, making it very beneficial to diabetics. A study also showed that sage can lower harmful cholesterol levels in the body.

Chakra Healing

When your seven chakras are balanced, they can benefit your body. Each chakra has its own role in providing healing to the mind and body. For instance, the third eye chakra can improve vision, reduce headaches and migraines, and treat sinus issues. The throat chakra provides healing to any issues in the throat area like sore throat, neck pain, and mouth issues. It can also help with ear infections and reduce shoulder pain as well. Balancing the heart chakra can help with heart problems, breast issues, asthma, allergies, immune diseases, and upper back pain. The solar plexus chakra can reduce blood pressure, improve digestion, and treat chronic fatigue. The navel chakra can help with fertility issues and reduce lower back pain.

Tools to Protect and Nurture Your Mental/Spiritual Body

Now that you have learned about the tools that can help protect and nurture your physical body, we will discuss tools that focus on your mental and spiritual well-being.

Journaling

Do you have a diary or a journal? If not, you'll get one after learning about the many benefits of journaling. We all experience negative thoughts and emotions every now and then. Keeping them bottled up is not good for your mind or spirit. Journaling allows you to release these thoughts, reducing stress and anxiety and giving you clarity. When you put whatever is bothering you in writing, it gives you a better perspective so you can find a solution to your problem. Additionally, writing down negative thoughts separates you from them so you can look at them from an objective point of view.

Once you clear your negative thoughts, you free up space for more positivity to enter your life, improving your mood and making you happier. It also helps you better understand yourself and all the changes you have been through. Journaling helps you reconnect and get reacquainted with yourself by learning about your strengths and weaknesses. What scares you? What do you like? What do you dislike? What are your hopes and dreams? All of these things you can learn about through journaling. Are you ready to go shopping for a new diary now?

Breathwork

We need a whole book to write about the many benefits of breathwork. Yes, there are that many. Breathwork helps with many mental issues like stress, anxiety, and depression. It also helps you manage your anger and deal with grief. Deep breathing can boost your energy, calm your brain, and keep you focused. This is because deep breathing slows down your heart rate, which helps you feel calm and relaxed.

Additionally, it makes you more mindful of the present moment. You become self-aware and only focused on the here and now. You are no longer obsessing over the past or worried about the future. Simply put, you live in the moment with no worries, which can boost your mood and make you happy.

Breathwork allows you to connect with yourself on a deeper level, making you accept and love who you are. We have all experienced traumatic experiences that live in our bodies, creating negative thoughts and emotions. Breathwork allows you to release these feelings through exhaling and the power of visualization.

Sage

We have talked about the benefits of sage as a food ingredient, but this herb's benefits don't end there. There is a known practice called "Burning sage" that began with Native Americans and is still relevant today. Burning sage helps improve your intuition, helps you solve spiritual dilemmas, and connects you with the spirit world. It can also release toxic energies from inside you or your home. If you have been through a traumatic experience or a fight has taken place in your house, consider burning sage to cleanse these negative energies.

When you get rid of negative energies, it can reduce your stress and anxiety and help improve your mood and overall well-being.

Cleaning

Most people regard cleaning as a chore that they just want to get done as quickly as possible. However, cleaning can have a huge impact on your mental health. A cluttered and untidy home can make you stressed and anxious. When you clean and declutter your house, you declutter your mind. Additionally, clean sheets promote better sleep quality which can, in turn, boost your mood. The act of cleaning itself can also impact your mental health as it reduces symptoms of depression and makes you more focused. Once you have finished cleaning your house and see the end results, it can do wonders for your mood.

Music

Who doesn't love music? When we want to celebrate, we turn on music and dance; when we are in love, we dance to slow love songs, and when we are sad, we find crying while listening to sad songs to be therapeutic. Music plays a huge role in our lives. Slow music helps calm our thoughts and reduces our stress and anxieties. Upbeat music can make us joyful and optimistic and help uplift our spirit. Listening to music can also be therapeutic as it reduces depressive thoughts.

Music also helps us understand our feelings better as sometimes we hear a lyric that can sum up our emotions, especially if we cannot find the right words to express ourselves. It also makes us feel less alone since we know someone out there experiences the same feelings we do.

Crystals

Crystals
https://www.pexels.com/photo/photo-of-assorted-crsytals-4040639

There are many types of crystals out there, and they all have amazing healing powers. Crystals reduce stress, increase your willpower, and help you to better understand your feelings. This helps you move on, provides you with inner strength, protects you from negative energies, provides clarity, and helps you process your grief. It also brings harmony to relationships, boosts your confidence, acts as a shield against negative vibes, encourages optimistic thoughts, releases negative emotions, and boosts your mood. Let the right one call out to you when shopping for a crystal. Once you find yourself pulled toward a specific crystal, then know that this is the one that will heal your body, mind, heart, and spirit.

Affirmations

We have provided you with positive affirmations in a previous chapter, but what do affirmations do to your mind and spirit? Affirmations are positive statements that reshape your thought patterns. The more you repeat them, the more you believe them, and they become facts replacing negative thoughts and self-doubt. Once positive energy and thoughts replace negative ones, you start to feel less stressed, happier, and grateful.

Memorize affirmations that apply to you and your needs and repeat them when you wake up, before bed, and during meditation. Make sure that your affirmations are realistic. Additionally, you should know that affirmations aren't magic, and you should still work for what you want and chase your dreams.

Speaking Up

As an HSP, you may find it difficult to speak up because you don't want to hurt someone's feelings. However, staying silent and not standing up for yourself can damage your mental health. So, speak up whenever you feel like it, especially if you deal with energy vampires who keep taking from you and draining your energy. Speaking up will increase your self-esteem, reduce tension, make you feel empowered, and improve your mental health. Even if you have different opinions from someone else, never be afraid to speak up and express them. Always celebrate and embrace your uniqueness.

Steering Clear of Energy Vampires

We have talked about the impact of energy vampires and toxic energies on our mental health. One of the best ways to protect your energy is to steer clear of energy vampires. When you avoid these people, you won't experience any of the negative emotions you usually feel after every interaction with them, like anger, exhaustion, discomfort, and many other negative emotions. As an empath who absorbs other people's emotions, you should always avoid energy vampires to protect yourself from absorbing their negativity which can affect your spirit, mental health, and overall well-being. So, stay away from negative people and surround yourself with positive ones who can lift you up and make you feel energized and upbeat after spending time with them. Life is too short to waste on people that burn and stress you out.

Setting Intentions

Setting intentions gives you purpose and helps you stay focused on what you want to achieve. It is a very simple practice where you repeat a small phrase that motivates and moves you to make your goal a reality. Setting intentions keeps you mindful, so you are only focused on your goal with no concern for the future or living with the regrets of the past. It opens your heart and allows you to be kind to yourself and others. For instance, if you wake up every day saying, "Today, I intend to choose forgiveness," you'll not hold grudges and will treat everyone with love and kindness. It can also bring positivity to your life as you begin your day by setting an intention of what exactly you'll feel, "I intend to be happy today and be consumed with positive energy." Setting intentions isn't a wish. It is a plan that motivates you to action.

Setting Healthy Boundaries

Setting boundaries is a form of self-care and is crucial to your well-being. It is a shield that protects your energy from being drained, and it also sets the tone for all your relationships as you communicate with people how you want to be treated. Setting boundaries allows you to take care of yourself since you aren't only focused on other people's needs while neglecting your own. When you take care of your needs, you become happier, more positive, and less resentful. Additionally, it helps you better understand yourself since you know what you accept and what you don't. It will also protect your energy since you won't waste it or your time on people who don't respect your boundaries.

When you say "no" to things that make you unhappy or uncomfortable, you become a happier and more positive person. Saying "no" to others is actually saying "yes" to your own happiness and well-being. You also avoid unnecessary stress and anxiety. Boundaries make you a confident person who doesn't tolerate disrespect or being walked over.

Toolbox of Different Practices to Protect Your Energy

- Meditation
- Exercise
- Walking in nature
- Hydration
- Eating clean food
- Consuming and burning sage
- Chakra healing
- Journaling
- Breathwork

- Cleaning
- Music
- Crystals
- Affirmations
- Speaking up
- Steering clear from energy vampires
- Setting intentions
- Setting healthy boundaries
- Practicing self-care

Once you start taking care of your body, mind, and spirit, you'll always feel positive and energized.

Chapter 9: Restoring and Nurturing Your Gifts

Every person has a unique set of gifts that gives them characteristic personality traits. HSPs also have their own gifts; the only difference is that they are often closer to the surface than others. This often means that your needs will be different and your life more challenging, and with a little bit of effort, you can turn these skills into your superpowers. This chapter is dedicated to restoring and nurturing your greatest gifts – high sensitivity and empathy. It will teach you how to use your ability to harness – energy and as a tool to form a meaningful connection with your environment. If you are willing to work on bringing out the positive side of your powers, you can achieve spiritual growth and the well-balanced life you deserve.

Highly Sensitive People and Empathy

The term highly sensitive people (or HSP) refers to individuals born with increased sensitivity in their nervous system. Their sensory organs have a much lower threshold than others, allowing them to react to a much broader range of emotional, physical, and spiritual stimulation. While this is often viewed as a negative trait, being too sensitive can be an extremely versatile tool in life.

Another gift an HSP often carries is empathy, a separate form of high sensitivity. An empath is a person who is even more attuned to the energy of their surroundings than most HSP. Apart from being more susceptible to all the stimuli emanating from the environment, the nervous system of an empath also has an unusually large number of mirror neurons. With the help of these neurons, empaths can feel emotions much more deeply.

As an empath, you have the uncanny ability to understand the feelings of those around you. This comes from the subconscious part of your mind, which prompts you to use your intuition – and listen to it. Being free to choose to go with your gut liberates your spirit and allows for much more creativity in your life.

It's important to note that not all HSP can feel the level of empathy to be labeled an empath. Both of these groups feel the need to empower others and live a simple life close to nature. However, as they have more introverted characteristics, HSP will prefer to do the latter and simply choose not to help others. Empaths, however, won't hesitate to lend a helping hand to anyone or anything in their environment. Empaths indeed tend to internalize the discomfort, which can lead to confusing them with your own.

The Benefits of Having Highly Sensitivity as a Gift

There are so many benefits to being a highly sensitive person or an empath. Your ability to tap into the emotions and energies of others can empower you to achieve your goals, avoid false people, and care for your loved ones. Here are some of the advantages of being an HSP that allow you to do all this.

Sensitivity to Sensory Details

Unlike the others, this trait is typically noted by the person displaying it, not that this makes it less significant. Since you process all the parts of the sensory information you receive more thoroughly, it allows you to notice some subtleties that other people may miss. Your brain will register and process every difference in shades and texture of the objects around you, the subtle differences in the fragrance of flowers, the richness of the flavor of the meals you are cooking, and many more sensory details in depth. This allows you to find joy in the simple things in life and respond to people's energies according to their vibe. No one will spot a liar before an HSP does. They can sense the negative energy in the tone of voice or the sudden changes in breathing.

Awareness of Nuances in Meaning

Because you are more aware of the nuances in meanings of what people say and do or what's happening in your nature, you can be more vigilant about making decisions regarding these actions. If necessary, you can act with incredible speed and accuracy simply because you detected a minor difference that could make taking immediate action worthwhile. Despite this, your attention to the details will make it far less likely for you to experience an error in judgment, no matter how rushed the decision may seem to be in the eyes of others. This is because your brain can process the possible outcome while it does the action itself.

Figuring Out Good Outcomes

Not only are you more likely to expect a good outcome from your actions, but you can also make it happen. HSPs, more than anyone else, know what positive difference emotions, such as satisfaction, joy, and happiness, can make in someone's life. No wonder they are keen to take action to make them a reality. You can use this gift to bring many positive moments into your life and build a new set of happy memories you can tap into when times are hard.

Semantic Memory

A person with a semantic memory can compare present and future situations with past experiences. This means that you can process any material on a deeper level and create a database of long-term memory of everything you have learned. You may have noticed that you have a higher aptitude for languages, easily conquering foreign vocals, terms, and phrases that others around you may struggle with. This is because your brain stores away the most important elements of any concept-based knowledge and can easily recall it whenever needed.

Unconscious Learning

Sometimes HSP can learn something even without realizing it. This is because you are so intuitive that you can take in and process high loads of information without even wanting to. You probably encountered a situation in the past where the solution to a problem just came to you even before you thought about it. If this sounds familiar to you, now you know that you must have learned the solution beforehand – you just didn't know that you did.

Higher Morals

HSPs are blessed with an unusually high level of conscientiousness. Whether you were raised with a specific set of moral values or not, deep down, you know what's wrong and what's right. You always try to show consideration toward people - even those who you can clearly sense are not being conscientious. You can make sure you or your possessions are never getting in someone else's way. This is also a great way to keep your valuables safe.

Greater Empathy

Sensing what those around you are feeling allows you to better understand them as individuals. A person may not show their emotions outward due to fear, shame, or other negative emotions, but you'll know how they feel and can help them if needed. Having greater empathy makes you a healer in a non-traditional way. You can always be there for your family and friends should they need someone to talk to about their problems or even advice on how to get professional help.

This makes you a better participant in your relationships and strengthens your bond with those you love, but it allows you to make new connections. Nothing establishes the foundation of relationships better than gaining a person's trust. As a result, you gain a much wider circle that knows they can rely on you anytime in the future, and they will also be there for you should you need them.

Self-Awareness

The people around you aren't the only ones to whom you are attuned emotionally. As an HSP, you are far more aware of your own emotional states than most people tend to be. This means that you'll notice if something is wrong much faster and are more likely to seek professional help. You have an innate ability to take proper care of your body and mind. So, unless you choose to ignore your intuition, you won't have any trouble maintaining good health.

You also have the capacity to express your emotions through artistic mediums. Whether you write, paint, make songs about them or act them out in a play - your emotions are a fertile ground of inspiration. Even if you do it as a pastime, your work will always be profound and full of meanings you wish to communicate to the rest of the world.

Introvert Personality Traits

One of the main reasons HSP finds solace in creativity and learning how to express themselves through the medium of art is because all of them have introverted tendencies. While empaths tend to display some extroverted traits, they still find it easier to express themselves through means other than speaking directly about their emotions. Not being able to talk about your emotions with your loved ones can be frustrating, particularly if you have no trouble listening to them. Nevertheless, you can still show them everything you feel through the art of your choice.

Sharp Fine Motor Movement

Your attention to detail also makes you a specialist at using your fine motor movement skills. These are the talents required to play instruments, draw, or create fine objects by hand. Sharper fine motor skills also allow you to excel in certain sports based on precise action and reaction times. In addition to being born with this ability, you can also hone it further by training the small muscle groups needed for the job to act in a perfectly synchronized fashion.

Contemplating Thought Processes

It's often said that HSPs tend to overthink everything in life, which may be true to a certain extent. You probably wondered why you think about certain things as much as you do. First of all, thinking about yourself doesn't occupy more of your brain than thinking about others does. It just ensures you aren't neglecting your mental well-being. Second, despite having a strong gut feeling about something, you can sometimes be distracted by other emotions, causing you to ignore your intuition. Reflecting on your thoughts can make you aware of mistakes like this, so you can avoid making them in the future.

Deeper Spiritual Consciousness

Whether you are devoted to a particular religion or not, you consider it essential to keep in touch with your spiritual needs. Nourishing your soul comes easily to you because you listen to its desires. You may also find yourself concerned about the spiritual needs of others and want to help them grow as well. You have the gift to teach them how to take a better approach to their lives, often discovering a new purpose for yours too along the way.

How to Restore and Nurture Empathy and High Sensitivity

Without psychic self-defense, your gifts are highly prone to different forms of psychic attacks, including intake of negative energy and encounters with psychic vampires. Apart from learning how to protect your energy with a shield, you may also want to take other precautions to avoid taking on the feelings and the issues of others. A great way to do this is by nourishing all the wonderful gifts you now know you possess. Making them into your superpower will allow you to defend yourself, ensure your feelings are your own, and heal from the confusion of taking on other people's energy. Here are some great ways to do that:

Accept Your Gifts

The first step on your journey should be accepting your gifts of empathy, sensitivity, and all the other wonderful skills you were born with. Think about them and ask yourself if they merit the negative light you have viewed them with until now. You may feel uncomfortable with the negative thoughts you've become so accustomed to; still, you have to think of everything they make you feel as being *empowering tools* to release your emotions.

Consider Where the Energy Comes From

More often than not, negative energy comes from a person you have a close relationship with. Because your feelings toward them tend to cloud your judgment, this can be a hard pill to swallow. That said, doing nothing hasn't made the negativity disappear until now. If anything, it probably made things worse. So, the obvious step after accepting your gifts is to acknowledge that you need to deal with them by channeling them in the right direction.

Protect Your Gifts

Now that you know that your sensitivity is a gift rather than a burden, it's time for you to learn how to protect it. Try releasing the thoughts and emotions you pick up through journaling to protect your feelings. Just write a few sentences in the morning or evening, and you'll soon feel much better about using your gifts. You can also write personalized affirmations to further remind yourself of their usefulness.

Set Boundaries

Setting boundaries is another excellent way to shield your energy. That said, this step is also one of the hardest ones you'll ever have to take as an HSP. For one, you need to make others aware of your intention to protect your energy. You must also consider that those around you may not like these boundaries. And if they can't respect the line you draw, your relationship will suffer. Try to talk to them about your need to do this and also explain that you need your highly sensitive nature honored.

You also need to make sure you are clear about your boundaries. To do this, you must take the time to observe each area of your life to see where your energy is being drained or if it's being tainted with negativity. Apart from specific people, toxic energy can also come from an environment. If it does, you should look into changing it as soon as possible to create a life that's a better fit for yourself.

Cleanse Your Energy with Physical Activity

There are various practices to cleanse your energy mentally, but none of them are as engaging as moving your body and making the energy move through it. Besides, following the previous steps can be exhausting mentally, so it's time for you to recharge your energy through some physical activity.

As an introvert, sports and other group activities may not work for you, but there are other things you can try. You can simply take a walk in the park after your lunch and breathe in the fresh air, letting it cleanse your energy. You can also dance away the negativity. Feel free to do this by yourself and include any movement you like.

Any movement that washes away the negativity and rejuvenates your energy can work. Speaking of washing, taking a bath or a shower after your workout is always a good idea. It will clear away all the remnants of toxicity that may still be clinging to your body.

Grounding Yourself in the Present

Above all, the most important time to focus on is the present. All the negativity you take regularly has to be properly processed and channeled away from your mind and body. This requires you to really stay grounded, which is only possible if you focus on what is happening now. The past memories can only guide you to a certain extent, and worrying about the future is not remotely helpful in this situation.

Practices that allow you to stay in the present will allow you to be calm, relaxed, and focused on your goals. Try to opt for a grounding exercise that can be performed outside, so you can also be close to nature. It will lend you its pure energy and provide the stability you need to stay in the present. Because it requires you to slow down your processing and filtering through stimuli and emotions, grounding yourself is one of the best ways to hone your sensitivity superpowers. Just make sure you are doing something you find fulfilling and not just doing it for the sake of doing it.

Use Your Gifts to Help Your Loved Ones

Now that you have empowered yourself with the best tools for processing negativity, it's time for you to try out your gifts on others. In the beginning, you may be unsure whether you'll be able to keep to these boundaries and respect other people's privacy. This is entirely normal, and it is the main reason you should start with people you have a loving relationship with. The way you'll need to channel the energy depends on the individual person, so it's much safer to practice it with someone who understands and accepts your gifts. Start by having a genuine conversation with friends and family members, empathize with them, and try to come up with a solution for whatever problem they may have in their life.

Give Back to Your Community

When you are comfortable using your gifts on your loved ones, you can take them to another level by giving back to the community. As introverts, HSPs often find it hard to assimilate into a larger community, so this will definitely be a big step for you. Not using your gifts to help out those in need would be a lost opportunity for personal growth, which is one of the requirements of having a healthy energy field.

Express Your Sensitivity through Art

HSPs have an innate ability to express themselves through art in a way they cannot do otherwise. So why not use this superpower to create something permanent by channeling all your energy into it? Giving handmade creations as a gift is one of the best ways to spread positivity around you and ensure everyone can remain happy and healthy, including yourself.

Letting go of the misconceptions about your sensitivity can be challenging. Society conditioned us to view sensitivity as a weakness when, in fact, it doesn't have to be at all. It can be your greatest strength, but only if you are willing to work on it. Understanding how to use your gifts can transform your life completely, making you feel safe, happy, and surrounded by people who care about you.

Chapter 10: 30-Day Challenge to Protect Your Energy

This chapter will find a 30-day challenge that can help you protect your energy. Each day of the challenge comes with a daily affirmation that will allow you to set your intention for the day. Make a mark at the bullet points to tick off the daily tasks you complete.

Day 1:

Today's Affirmation: *"I am responsible for the quality of my relationships."*

- **Say "no."** Say no to any requests you don't feel like doing. Prioritize your own needs and wishes.

- **Detach.** Be mindful of where you direct your energy and thoughts, and only concern yourself with what affects you. As an empath, you'll inevitably sense the feelings of others. The trick here is to force yourself not to do anything about it because once you decide that you need to help "fix" things for them, it becomes your burden.

- **Do the Body Scan Meditation.** Refer to chapter 2 for instructions. This meditation will help you become aware of all the sensations in your body, whether they're physical, emotional, or thought-related.

Day 2:

Today's Affirmation: *"I release the past and fully open my heart to the present."*

- **Go for a long walk in nature.** Immerse yourself in the experience. Take notice of the different hues you see, listen closely to the animals, and smell the rain, flowers, and wet tree trunks. Feel the crisp air on your arms and face, and breathe deeply.

- **Practice Yoga.** You can choose any pose you want. However, we recommend the mountain pose, especially if you're a beginner. It's easy to do and can help increase your body awareness. It can also help improve your posture and alignment.

  Stand up straight with your feet flat on the floor. Allow your big toes to touch but leave your heels slightly parted. Lift your chest up while pushing your shoulders down. Your palms should be facing forward. Slightly tuck in your chin and extend the crown of your head. Breathe through your nose while keeping your throat constricted. Do this for about 5 to 10 breaths.

- **Journal.** Think about everything that's bothering you and reflect on your negative emotions. Write down everything that's on your mind. Journaling can help you release your emotions and will allow you to connect with your feelings.

Day 3:

Today's Affirmation: *"I grant myself permission to heal."*

- **Drink water.** Drinking a glass of water first thing in the morning can help boost your mood, mental performance, and metabolism.

- **Eat plenty of greens.** Honor your body by eating a healthy and hearty bowl of salad.

- **Exercise for 20 to 30 minutes.** You can do any form of exercise you like. For example, watch and follow dancing videos or do circuit training workouts at home.

- **Practice deep breathing.** Breathe deeply for 2 to 3 minutes. You can close your eyes and bring awareness to your bodily sensations.

- **Use essential oils.** Take a long relaxing bath and use a calming essential oil like lavender or frankincense.

- **Do light stretches.** Do light stretching exercises before you go to bed.

Day 4:

Today's Affirmation: *"I experience happiness in all that I do."*

- **Be optimistic.** Write down how you want your day to go when you wake up. You don't need to include details. Just mention the emotions you want to feel, like joy, excitement, happiness, etc. Write them in the present tense, avoid negative statements, and start the statements with "I" (just like how you'd write an affirmation).

- **Meditate.** Practice any form of meditation you want to for 5 minutes. You can refer to chapter 2 for examples and instructions.

- **Look at the silver lining.** Try to point out as many good things throughout your day as possible. If something unfortunate happens, search for the upside and point it out, no matter how small it is. Make this a habit.

- **Listen to upbeat music.** Play happy music while you're getting ready, on your way to work, while you're cooking, etc.

- **Exit negative conversations.** Being around people can be overwhelming enough for you. Don't be afraid to exit negative and stressful conversations.

Day 5:

Today's Affirmation: *"I am capable of unconditional love."*

- **Play with a baby, pet a dog or cat.** This will help boost your mood and lower stress hormone levels.

- **Do a random act of kindness.**

- **Smile at a stranger.**

- **Forgive someone who hurt you.** Write down how this person hurt you (it could be yourself) and how you feel about it. Burn the paper and let it go. You don't need to talk to them again. Forgiving them from within allows you to make peace with the situation and will help you move on.

Day 6:

Today's Affirmation: *"I let go of all my pain."*

- **Meditate.** Meditate for 5 minutes.

- **Exercise.** Stretch or do a light form of exercise for 15 minutes.

- **Heal your energy.** Refer to chapter 8 for ideas. Carrying a citrine crystal can help you practice mindfulness. You can also visit a reiki master or a professional massage practitioner for a healing session.

- **Take naps.** If you feel tired throughout your day, don't resist the need for a nap.

Day 7:

Today's Affirmation: *"I feel at peace with each breath I take."*

- **Practice deep breathing.** Breathe deeply for 2 minutes.

- **Take a break from technology.** Avoid using social media and technological devices throughout your day.

  Note: You can switch days if day 7 doesn't fall on a weekend. You may need to check your email or be online for work purposes.

- **Detach.** Be mindful of where you direct your energy and thoughts, and only concern yourself with what affects you.

Day 8:

Today's Affirmation: *"I let go of the need to stay in control."*

- **Practice yoga.** We recommend the upward-facing dog pose for day 8. To start this pose, you need to lie down on your stomach. While inhaling, straighten your arms and lift your chest upward. Open your heart. The top of your feet should be flat on the ground (heels upward and toes flat down and back). Bring your thighs and knees off the mat. Stay in this position for 3 to 5 breaths.

- **Let it be.** Don't try to control certain outcomes throughout the day and embrace the natural flow of things.

- **Turn negative "What Ifs" into positive ones.** "What if I mess up?" -> "What if it all goes as planned?"

Day 9:

Today's Affirmation: *"I am fully open to giving and receiving love."*

- **Practice self-love.** Write down three things you genuinely love about yourself. Remind yourself of these qualities throughout your day.

- **Be expressive.** Thank and appreciate the people you love. Show gratitude.

- **Stand your ground.** Stand your ground and express yourself even when someone challenges your beliefs.

- **Embrace your helpful nature.** If you sense that someone needs help, ask what you can do for them. Remember not to go out of your way or do something that compromises your own mental, emotional, and physical well-being. Learn to help within reasonable limits.

Day 10:

Today's Affirmation: *"I am thankful for all the blessings in my life."*

- **Practice gratitude.** Think of all the things, qualities, and people you're thankful for.

- **Meditate.** Meditate for 5 minutes.

- **Go for a long walk in nature.** Be fully present and express your gratitude for all the good things in life. Allow yourself to feel moved by the beauty of your surroundings.

- **Give back.** Plant a seed, help clean your neighborhood, help someone, or need, or give back to a friend.

Day 11:

Today's Affirmation: *"I take a step toward reaching my goals every single day."*

- **Drink a glass of water.** Drink a glass of water in the morning to flush out the toxins and boost your mood and concentration.

- **Schedule your day.** Write down a to-do list so you can plan out the day ahead.

- **Exercise.** Do your favorite form of exercise for 30 minutes.

- **Do something you've been avoiding.** Whether it's cleaning out your office space or organizing your closet, it's time to finally do a task you've been avoiding.

- **Practice visualization.** Take 10 to 15 minutes to visualize the future you desire with all its details.

Day 12:

Today's Affirmation: *"I am safe. I am protected. A shield of positive energy surrounds me."*

- **Do an emotional release.** Think about your emotions and identify the ones that belong to you and those you absorbed from others. Write it all down in your journal.

- **Meditate.** Meditate for 5 minutes.

- **Take a break.** Take the day off from work and allow yourself to slack off chores.

- **Burn sage.** Burning sage can elevate your mood, remove toxins and bacteria from the room, and reduce stress and anxiety levels.

- **Do something fun.** Practice a hobby, watch a funny movie, go for a walk, etc...

Day 13:

Today's Affirmation: *"I am open to receiving unexpected opportunities."*

- **Drink a glass of water.** Drink a glass of water in the morning to set the tone for the day.

- **Reset your awareness.** Refer to chapter 2 for instructions on how to do this meditative practice. Do it multiple times during different experiences.

- **Adopt an optimistic mindset.** Go about your day expecting great things to happen out of the blue.

- **Get outside of your comfort zone.** Do something you've always wanted to do but never had the chance to.

- **Take chances.** Is there an attractive opening at a company you've been reluctant to apply to? Go for it!

Day 14:

Today's Affirmation: *"I attract kind and like-minded people."*

- **Have meaningful conversations.** Small talk can be draining for anyone. Try to avoid it and opt for meaningful conversations instead.

- **Be selective.** Be selective when it comes to choosing who to spend your time with. Avoid hanging out with negative or judgmental people.

- **Say goodbye.** Let go of those who no longer serve you. Make your peace with this decision and be certain that this is for your own good.

- **Think before you speak.** Choosing your words carefully and avoiding negative talk is a good habit to build.

- **Do a random act of kindness.**

Day 15:

Today's Affirmation: *"I prioritize my mind, body, and spirit."*

- **Practice deep breathing.** Breathe deeply and mindfully for 2 minutes.

- **Have a nutritious breakfast.** Eat a balanced breakfast to boost your concentration and energy levels.

- **Drink enough water.** Make sure you're drinking enough water throughout your day.

- **Exercise.** Do your favorite form of exercise for 45 to 60 minutes.

- **Reward yourself.** Do something that makes you happy. Reward yourself for making it halfway through!

Day 16:

Today's Affirmation: *"My choice to be happy keeps me in optimal health."*

- **Meditate.** Meditate for 10 minutes.

- **Avoid stimulants.** Instead of managing your high sensitivity during stressful situations, take a break for the day and avoid stimulants altogether.

- **Exercise.** Work out for 15 minutes.

- **Laugh.** Hang out with people or watch movies that make you laugh.

Day 17:

Today's Affirmation: *"I realize these circumstances are an opportunity to help me grow."*

- **Practice the Meditative Walk technique.** Refer to chapter 2 for instructions. This technique can both help raise your awareness and stay focused on the present moment.
- **Stretch.** Stretch your body for 15 minutes.
- **Practice visualization.** Take a few minutes to visualize the future you desire.
- **Broaden your knowledge.** Read something educational or start learning a new skill.

Day 18:

Today's Affirmation: *"I have the power to shape the reality I want."*

- **Do a yoga flow.** Search for a step-by-step yoga flow video for beginners on YouTube and do it.
- **Go offline.** Take a break from technology and social media for the day.
- **Get creative.** Practice any creative activity. Draw, paint, dance, write, bake, etc.
- **Practice one of your hobbies.**

Day 19:

Today's Affirmation: *"I don't allow fear and self-doubt to stand in the way of my goals and desires."*

- **Practice a grounding technique.** Choose any grounding technique you like and practice it.

Suggestion: 54321 grounding method.

Bring awareness to your breath, and then search for five things you can see, four things you can touch, three things you can hear, two things you can smell, and one thing you can taste.

- Exercise. Work out for 30 minutes.
- Get over a fear. Take steps toward overcoming a fear.
- Let go. Let go of the need to be in control.

Day 20:

Today's Affirmation: *"I can feel my spirit being recharged every time I connect with nature."*

- **Eat your greens.** Focus on fueling your body with fruits and vegetables.

- **Walk outside.** Take a 20-minute walk in nature.

- **Embrace natural light and air.** Open all the windows in your home, allowing fresh air and light to flow in.

- **Reset your awareness.** Do the Reset Your Awareness mindfulness technique.

Day 21:

Today's Affirmation: *" I am getting closer to achieving my goals every day."*

- **Meditate.** Meditate for 10 minutes.

- **Reflect.** Reflect on how far you've made it through this routine, the progress you're making at managing your high sensitivity, and the steps you took toward achieving your goals.

- **Practice self-compassion.** Express your gratitude, compassion, and appreciation toward yourself.

- **Be proud.** Allow yourself to feel proud of all your achievements.

Day 22:

Today's Affirmation: *"I am grateful for all my experiences."*

- **Count your blessings.** Write down three good things in your life.

- **Express your gratitude.** Thank your friends and family, and most importantly, yourself.

- **Make use of social media.** Use the power of social media to spread positivity and do good.

Day 23:

Today's Affirmation: *"I love and accept myself deeply."*

- **Practice a grounding technique.** Do the 5-4-3-2-1 grounding technique or choose any other method.

- **Practice Yoga.** Check Day 2 for instructions on the Mountain pose.

- **Release your thoughts and emotions.** Give yourself the space to feel all your emotions and reflect on them. Embrace all your feelings and speak your truth.
- **Carry a healing stone.** Amazonite will help you manage emotional turmoil and encourage you to follow your passion.

Day 24:

Today's Affirmation: *"I declutter my life to create space for receiving the support and comfort that I need."*

- **Organize your schedule.** Prioritize tasks from most to least important and eliminate things that are no longer essential. A messy schedule can trigger your high sensitivity.
- **Declutter your home.** A messy home can act as an overwhelming stimulant. Donate the things you no longer need.
- **Detach.** Let go of thoughts, people, emotions, and events that don't serve you anymore.

Day 25:

Today's Affirmation: *"I am independent and self-sufficient."*

- **Meditate.** Meditate for 5 minutes.
- **Stretch.** Stretch your body for 10 minutes.
- **Say "no."** Prioritize your well-being.
- **Work on self-development.** Practice a skill or a talent.

Day 26:

Today's Affirmation: *"I know that everything in my life is unfolding perfectly."*

- **Send it back.** If you receive unwanted thoughts and emotions, you have to remember that they most likely aren't yours. You probably absorbed them from someone else. Take a moment to identify what you're thinking and feeling. If they're not yours, send them back.
- **Practice deep breathing.** Breathe deeply for 2 to 3 minutes.
- **Exercise for 20 to 30 minutes.** Practice any form of exercise you like.

Day 27:

Today's Affirmation: *"I am willing to be at peace with myself."*

- **Practice deep breathing.** Breathe deeply for 2 to 3 minutes.
- **Do an emotional release.** Journal your thoughts and emotions.
- **Practice self-care.** Take a long relaxing bath, have a spa day, or burn calming essential oils.
- **Do light stretches.** Do light stretches before you go to bed.

Day 28:

Today's Affirmation: *"My happiness comes from within me."*

- **Listen to upbeat music.** Play happy music whenever you get the chance to.
- **Do the Body Scan Meditation.** Refer to chapter 2 for instructions.
- **Meditate.** Meditate for 10 minutes.

Day 29:

Today's Affirmation: *"I'm willing to see things differently."*

- **Burn sage.** Burn sage to elevate your mood.
- **Practice visualization.** Take 10 to 15 minutes to visualize the future you desire.
- **Drink enough water.** Make sure you're drinking enough water throughout the day.

Day 30:

Today's Affirmation: *"I create new routines based on the goals I wish to achieve."*

- **Practice deep breathing.** Breathe deeply and mindfully for 2 minutes.
- **Meditate.** Practice any form of meditation you want for 5 minutes.
- **Reflect.** Reflect on the past 30 days. How did your life change? Do you believe you can manage your high sensitivity more efficiently now?
- **Reward yourself.** Reward yourself for making it to the end of the challenge.

Dealing with your high sensitivity can get very challenging at times. However, this fun 30-day routine can help you stay on track so you can protect your energy. Turning these tasks into habits can help you transform your life.

Conclusion

Everyone has been told that they're overly sensitive or emotional at some point in their lives. It's also normal to be accused of taking things too personally when you react differently than other people. Maybe you've always been too sensitive when it came to loud noises, physical interactions, and bright lights, but you always saw it as a mere quirk. Perhaps you never thought that it could actually mean something more until you picked up this book.

Highly sensitive individuals are widely misunderstood. They are often mislabeled as introverts or thought to be too dramatic. HSPs are often bullied, criticized, and viewed as weak. Physical and emotional strength, persistence, and resilience are glorified, while compassionate, sensitive, and generous individuals are taken advantage of.

The lack of awareness of high sensitivity in society can hurt HSPs significantly. It can make it hard for them to actively participate in the community, but it can make it hard for them to understand themselves. Being highly sensitive, as opposed to popular belief, is not something you need to hide, fix, or be ashamed of. Sensitivity can put individuals at an advantage. It can make them more appreciative, creative, empathetic, and intelligent. Highly sensitive individuals are blessed with incredible intrapersonal and intuitive skills.

There's a common misconception that HSPs are emotionally sensitive and take things to heart. Being a highly sensitive person, however, goes beyond feelings and emotions. The term is used to describe individuals who are more sensitive to mental, physical, and emotional stimuli than the average person. It's also important to note that high sensitivity is a personality trait, just like extraversion, introversion, creativity, and friendliness. It's not a mental ailment that needs to be fixed. Like every other characteristic, high sensitivity comes with disadvantages when mismanaged.

Now that you've read this book, you can tell for sure whether you are a highly sensitive person or an empath. This will help you take the right approach and determine the steps you need to take to maintain your mental, spiritual, physical, and emotional well-being. You understand the different challenges you may face in life and the various techniques you can use to cope with these situations. The book also gives its readers insight into the concept of energies and the chakra system, making it a great place to start for individuals who wish to embark on their energy and chakra healing journey.

Chapters 4 and 5 of the book should make it easier for you to determine toxic energies in your life and learn how to protect yourself from them. You'll know the different types of energy vampires and how you can interact with them efficiently without compromising your own well-being. The last few chapters are targeted at helping you practice self-care and set boundaries. These chapters provide different tools and techniques you can use to protect your personal energy and replenish it after an energy vampire has depleted it. Finally, the 30-day challenge at the end of the book can help you take steps toward changing your life.

Here's another book by Mari Silva that you might like

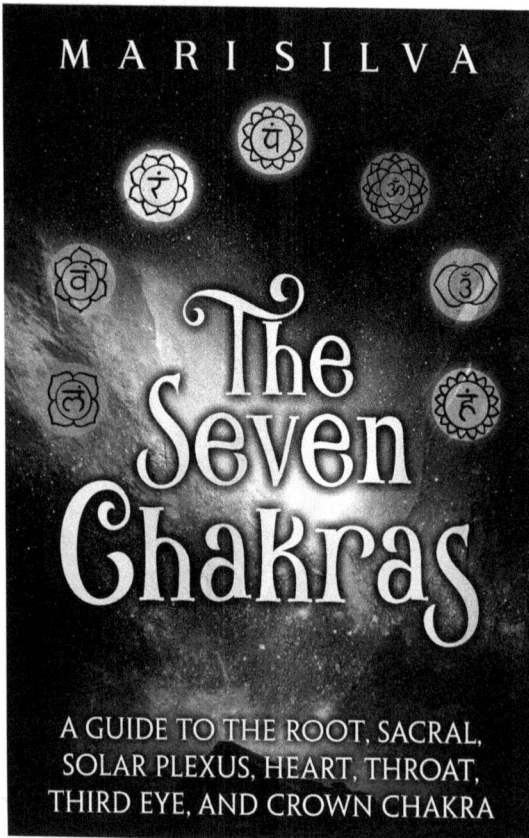

MARI SILVA

The Seven Chakras

A GUIDE TO THE ROOT, SACRAL, SOLAR PLEXUS, HEART, THROAT, THIRD EYE, AND CROWN CHAKRA

Your Free Gift
(only available for a limited time)

Thanks for getting this book! If you want to learn more about various spirituality topics, then join Mari Silva's community and get a free guided meditation MP3 for awakening your third eye. This guided meditation mp3 is designed to open and strengthen ones third eye so you can experience a higher state of consciousness. Simply visit the link below the image to get started.

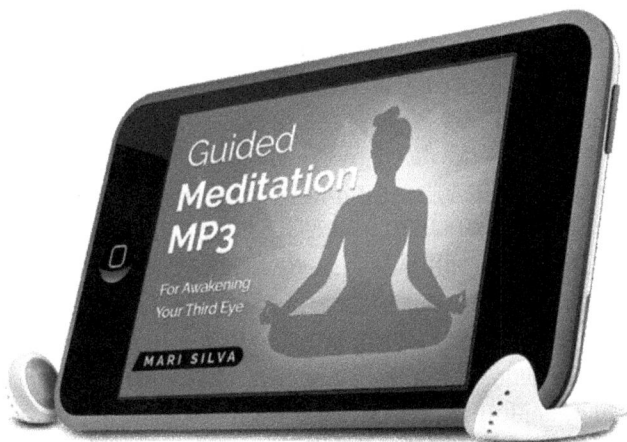

https://spiritualityspot.com/meditation

Bibliography

Sacks, B., & Religion News Service. (2014, May 16). Reiki goes mainstream: Spiritual touch practice now commonplace in hospitals. Washington Post (Washington, D.C.: 1974). https://www.washingtonpost.com/national/religion/reiki-goes-mainstream-spiritual-touch-practice-now-commonplace-in-hospitals/2014/05/16/9e92223a-dd37-11e3-a837-8835df6c12c4_story.html

Types of complementary and alternative medicine. (2019, November 19). Hopkinsmedicine.Org. https://www.hopkinsmedicine.org/health/wellness-and-prevention/types-of-complementary-and-alternative-medicine

Adam, B. (2018, November 5). What is a Reiki attunement? My Blog. https://www.pathwayshealing.com/what-is-a-reiki-attunement/

Administrator, R. (2014, October 15). What is Reiki? Reiki. https://www.reiki.org/faqs/what-reiki

Bedosky, L., & Laube, J. (n.d.). Reiki: How this energy healing works and its health benefits. EverydayHealth.Com. https://www.everydayhealth.com/reiki/

Cauldrons, & Cupcakes. (2019, January 22). Are You A Sensitive, Intuitive, Psychic, or Empathic Soul? Here's a Checklist to help you find out! Cauldrons and Cupcakes. https://cauldronsandcupcakes.com/2019/01/23/are-you-a-sensitive-intuitive-psychic-or-empathic-soul-heres-a-checklist-to-help-you-find-out/

Cronkleton, E. (2018, June 21). Reiki: Benefits, what to expect, crystals, finding a practitioner. Healthline. https://www.healthline.com/health/reiki

Daly, A. (2019, April 22). Reiki might actually be worth A try if you're in pain. Women's Health. https://www.womenshealthmag.com/health/a27155104/what-is-reiki/

Everything you need to know about reiki symbols & their meanings. (2018, May 8). Mindbodygreen. https://www.mindbodygreen.com/articles/reiki-symbols-meanings/

How does Reiki work? (n.d.). Taking Charge of Your Health & Wellbeing. https://www.takingcharge.csh.umn.edu/explore-healing-practices/reiki/how-does-reiki-work

IARP. (2014, April 20). History of Reiki: Read about the origin and traditions of Reiki. IARP. https://iarp.org/history-of-reiki/

Luna, A. (2016, June 6). 30 signs you're born to be a spiritual healer. LonerWolf. https://lonerwolf.com/spiritual-healer/

Marcovigil, Giselle, Sam, Brown, S., Robert, Lisa, & K. (2020, June 26). How to tell if you are psychic? 6 signs you are A psychic medium. The Black Feather Intuitive. https://www.theblackfeatherintuitive.com/how-to-tell-if-you-are-psychic/

Naicker, X. (2021, September 6). 7 signs you're a healer and not just sensitive (updated in 2022). Mysticmag.Com; MysticMag. https://www.mysticmag.com/psychic-reading/signs-you-might-be-a-healer/

Nunez, K. (2020, August 24). Reiki principles and how to use them to boost well-being. Healthline. https://www.healthline.com/health/reiki-principles

Reiki Attunement - the process and the purpose. (2018, January 8). Centre of Excellence. https://www.centreofexcellence.com/reiki-attunement-process-purpose/

Rohan, E. (2022, May 20). Today's menopause solutions Aren't your mom's hot-flash remedies (I know because I asked mine). Well+Good. https://www.wellandgood.com/menopause-solutions-phenology/

Star, D. B. (2015). What Is Reiki? Createspace Independent Publishing Platform.

What is Reiki, and Does it Really Work? (2021, August 30). Cleveland Clinic. https://health.clevelandclinic.org/reiki/

(N.d.-a). Yourlegacyproject.Com. https://yourlegacyproject.com/10-signs-you-are-a-healer/

(N.d.-b). Com.Au. https://www.bodyandsoul.com.au/mind-body/10-surprising-signs-that-you-might-be-psychic/news-story/7220ada2fd93f329915bbaa529a78eb6

Biernacki, L. (2019). Subtle body. In Transformational Embodiment in Asian Religions (pp. 108–127). Routledge.

Davis, F. (2021, March 3). 11 ways to enhance your life force energy: Tap into the best version of you. Cosmic Cuts. https://cosmiccuts.com/blogs/healing-stones-blog/life-force-energy

Evolution Yoga. (2019, August 27). Chanting the chakra sounds and the nervous system. Evolution Physical Therapy and Yoga. https://evolutionvt.com/chanting-the-chakra/

Flinn, A. (2021, July 19). Your guide to auras: What they are & what to expect during A reading. Mindbodygreen. https://www.mindbodygreen.com/0-25407/what-is-an-aura-and-how-can-you-see-yours.html

Holland, K. (2022, January 5). What is an aura? 16 FAQs about seeing auras, colors, layers, and more. Healthline. https://www.healthline.com/health/what-is-an-aura

How to make an energy ball of chi. (2011, April 28). LEAFtv. https://www.leaf.tv/articles/how-to-make-an-energy-ball-of-chi/

Jain, R. (2019, June 13). Complete guide to 7 chakras & their effects. Arhanta Yoga Ashrams. https://www.arhantayoga.org/blog/7-chakras-introduction-energy-centers-effect/

Jain, R. (2020a, August 24). Muladhara Chakra, Root Chakra - complete guide. Arhanta Yoga Ashrams. https://www.arhantayoga.org/blog/all-you-need-to-know-about-muladhara-chakra-root-chakra/

Jain, R. (2020b, August 26). Svadhishthana - Sacral Chakra: All you need to know. Arhanta Yoga Ashrams. https://www.arhantayoga.org/blog/svadhishthana-chakra-all-you-need-to-know-about-the-sacral-chakra/

Jain, R. (2020c, September 3). Manipura Chakra: Healing powers of Solar Plexus Chakra. Arhanta Yoga Ashrams. https://www.arhantayoga.org/blog/manipura-chakra-healing-powers-of-the-solar-plexus-chakra/

Jain, R. (2020d, September 16). Anahata Chakra - Heart Chakra: Self-realization through love. Arhanta Yoga Ashrams. https://www.arhantayoga.org/blog/anahata-chakra-heart-chakra-self-realization-through-love/

Jain, R. (2020e, September 22). Vishuddha Chakra: How to balance your Throat Chakra. Arhanta Yoga Ashrams. https://www.arhantayoga.org/blog/vishuddha-chakra-balance-how-to-balance-your-throat-chakra/

Jain, R. (2020f, October 8). Crown chakra: The divine energy of Sahasrara chakra. Arhanta Yoga Ashrams. https://www.arhantayoga.org/blog/crown-chakra-divine-energy-of-sahasrara-chakra/

Lindberg, S. (2020, August 24). What are chakras? Meaning, location, and how to unblock them. Healthline. https://www.healthline.com/health/what-are-chakras

Are you an HSP or Empath. What's the difference? (n.d.). Empathdiary.Com https://www.empathdiary.com/messages/are-you-an-empath

Bradberry, M. (2021, October 7). 7 common problems you might be facing as a highly sensitive person (and what to do about them) — living better lives counseling LLC living better lives. Living Better Lives Counseling LLC.

https://www.livingbetterlivesnwa.com/blog/2021/10/5/5-common-problems-you-might-be-facing-as-a-highly-sensitive-person-and-what-to-do-about-them

Collins, M. (2020, October 7). The top 7 challenges of highly sensitive people, according to a therapist. Highly Sensitive Refuge. https://highlysensitiverefuge.com/top-7-challenges-of-highly-sensitive-people-according-to-a-therapist

Funniest Empath Quiz & More. (n.d.). Empathdiary.Com. https://www.empathdiary.com/quiz

Managing highly sensitive people. (n.d.). Mindtools.Com.

https://www.mindtools.com/pages/article/managing-highly-sensitive-people.htm

Migala, J. (2021, November 11). If you're a highly sensitive person, you experience the world differently—here's what it means. Health.Com. https://www.health.com/condition/mental-health-conditions/highly-sensitive-person-empath

Parpworth-Reynolds, C. (2020, May 13). 10 famous empaths – some of these may surprise you. Subconscious Servant. https://subconsciousservant.com/famous-empaths

QuizExpo. (2021a, February 15). Empath test. 100% accurate quiz reveals if you are an empath. Quiz Expo. https://www.quizexpo.com/am-i-an-empath-test

QuizExpo. (2021b, September 16). Highly Sensitive Person Test. 100% accurate quiz. Quiz

Expo. https://www.quizexpo.com/highly-sensitive-person-test

Sólo, A. (2020, June 17). The difference between introverts, empaths, and highly sensitive people. Highly Sensitive Refuge. https://highlysensitiverefuge.com/empaths-highly-sensitive-people-introverts

What type of details usually caught your attention? (2021, September 11). Quiz Expo. https://www.quizexpo.com/wpqquestionpnt/what-type-of-details-usually-caught-your-attention

Can mindfulness exercises help me? (2020, September 15). Mayo Clinic.

https://www.mayoclinic.org/healthy-lifestyle/consumer-health/in-depth/mindfulness-exercises/art-20046356

Scott, E. (n.d.-a). How highly sensitive people can reduce stress in their lives. Verywell Mind https://www.verywellmind.com/ways-to-cope-with-stress-when-highly-sensitive-4126398

Daniels, E. (2021, September 16). Why so many people wonder, "are Highly Sensitive people psychic?" Dr. Elayne Daniels. https://www.drelaynedaniels.com/why-so-many-people-wonder-are-highly-sensitive-people-psychic

Holland, K. (2022, January 5). What is an aura? 16 FAQs about seeing auras, colors, layers, and more. Healthline. https://www.healthline.com/health/what-is-an-aura

Jon Canas, P. (2021, September 6). The seven layers of the aura and how they relate to the seven chakras —. PHYTO5 Swiss Quantum Energetic Skincare. https://www.phyto5.us/blog-1/the-seven-layers-of-the-aura-and-how-they-relate-to-the-seven-chakras8/31/2021

Lee, P. by A. (2022, April 7). Let's talk energy: Understanding the world of Auras. Beyogi. https://beyogi.com/inside-the-world-of-auras

Lui, H. C. (2016, June 27). Know your Aura and seven chakras. Patch.

https://patch.com/massachusetts/medfield/know-your-aura-seven-chakras

What are auric fields and chakras? (2016, November 15). Suzanne Worthley.

https://sworthley.com/energy-healing/auric-fields-chakras

4 benefits of healthy relationships. (2019, August 3). Acenda. https://acendahealth.org/4-benefits-of-healthy-relationships

5 reasons studies say you have to choose your friends wisely. (n.d.). Psychology Today. https://www.psychologytoday.com/us/blog/what-mentally-strong-people-dont-do/201504/5-reasons-studies-say-you-have-to-choose-your-friends

Brennan, T. (2021, July 22). Affirmations in relationships. Vertellis.

https://vertellis.com/blogs/all/affirmations-in-relationships

Groth, A. (2012, July 24). You're the average of the five people you spend the most time with. Insider. https://www.businessinsider.com/jim-rohn-youre-the-average-of-the-five-people-you-spend-the-most-time-with-2012-7

Meyerowitz, A. (2019, August 1). Toxic people: 7 warning signs a person is toxic. Red Online. https://www.redonline.co.uk/health-self/self/a28577908/signs-a-person-is-toxic

Pangilinan, J. (2021, February 25). 35 relationship affirmations to grow your love together. Happier Human. https://www.happierhuman.com/relationship-affirmations

Raypole, C. (2019, November 21). How to deal with toxic people: 17 tips. Healthline. https://www.healthline.com/health/how-to-deal-with-toxic-people

Sharie Stines, P. D. (2020, March 26). How to protect yourself from others negative energy. Psych Central. https://psychcentral.com/pro/recovery-expert/2020/03/how-to-protect-yourself-from-others-negative-energy

Desy, P. L. (n.d.). Psychic vampires: Who are they and how do you avoid them? Learn Religions https://www.learnreligions.com/how-a-psychic-vampire-attack-happens-1724677

Jeffrey, S. (2019, January 3). The ultimate guide to energy vampires [everything you need to know]. Scott Jeffrey. https://scottjeffrey.com/emotional-energy-vampires

Melody. (2022, February 10). 3 types of Energy vampires and how to deal with them. Melody Wilding. https://melodywilding.com/3-types-of-energy-vampires-and-how-to-deal-with-them

15 simple self-care ideas for your morning routine. (2018, August 16). Real Food Whole Life. https://realfoodwholelife.com/selfcare/simplified-self-care-for-your-morning-routine

Andersen, N. (2018, July 23). 20 self-care ideas for highly sensitive people. Highly Sensitive Refuge. https://highlysensitiverefuge.com/self-care-ideas-for-highly-sensitive-people

April Snow, L. (2017, October 3). How to Set Boundaries as an HSP —. Expansive Heart Psychotherapy. https://www.expansiveheart.com/blog/how-to-set-boundaries-as-an-hsp

April Snow, L. (2019, March 27). Why Highly Sensitive People need meaningful self-care —. Expansive Heart Psychotherapy. https://www.expansiveheart.com/blog/highly-sensitive-self-care

Bjelland, J. (2021, July 13). How to set healthy boundaries as an HSP and improve your relationships. Julie Bjelland. https://www.juliebjelland.com/hsp-blog/healthy-boundaries-and-saying-no

Elizabeth Earnshaw, L. (2019, July 20). 6 types of boundaries you deserve to have (and how to maintain them). Mindbodygreen. https://www.mindbodygreen.com/articles/six-types-of-boundaries-and-what-healthy-boundaries-look-like-for-each

How to set boundaries when you're A Highly Sensitive Person. (2020, December 22). Thought Catalog. https://thoughtcatalog.com/vanessa-dewsbury/2020/12/how-to-set-boundaries-when-youre-a-highly-sensitive-person

How to use meditation to boost your energy (according to meditation teacher). (2021, May 18).

FitOn – #1 Free Fitness App, Stop Paying for Home Workouts. https://fitonapp.com/wellness/meditation-for-energy

Lawler, M., & Laube, J. (n.d.-a). How to start a self-care routine you'll follow. EverydayHealth.Com. https://www.everydayhealth.com/self-care/start-a-self-care-routine

Mackenzie-Smith, K. (2022, January 29). How to actually set better boundaries — the HSP way. Highly Sensitive Refuge. https://highlysensitiverefuge.com/how-to-actually-set-better-boundaries-as-an-hsp

ruikangma. (2021, July 1). Setting Boundaries: A healthy and Sustainable Boundaries.

International Coach Academy. https://coachcampus.com/coach-portfolios/research-papers/setting-boundaries

Scott, E. (n.d.). How proper self-care can reduce your stress levels. Verywell Mind.

https://www.verywellmind.com/importance-of-self-care-for-health-stress-management-3144704

Self-care for empaths: 6 energy-protecting strategies. (2020, May 31). Female Mind Unleashed. https://femalemindunleashed.com/self-care-empaths

Self-care practices I have discovered as A Highly Sensitive Person. (n.d.). Wellness

Minneapolis. https://www.wellnessminneapolis.com/articles/self-care-practices-i-have-discovered-as-a-highly-sensitive-person

Setting boundaries: The yes is as important as the no. (n.d.). Routledge.Com.

https://www.routledge.com/blog/article/setting-boundaries-the-yes-is-as-important-as-the-no

(N.d.). Newharbinger.Com.

https://www.newharbinger.com/blog/spirituality/boundaries-a-guide-for-empaths-and-sensitives

5 key benefits of setting intentions. (n.d.). Silk + Sonder.

https://www.silkandsonder.com/blogs/news/5-key-benefits-of-setting-intentions

5 positive effects music has on your mental health. (2020, February 10). Open Minds. https://www.openminds.org.au/news/5-positive-effects-music-mental-health

9 simple ways to make meditation a daily habit. (n.d.). Headspace.Com.

Bailey, K. (2018, July 31). 5 powerful health benefits of journaling.

Intermountainhealthcare.Org.

https://intermountainhealthcare.org/blogs/topics/live-well/2018/07/5-powerful-health-benefits-of-journaling

Do affirmations work? Yes, but there's a catch. (2020, September 1). Healthline. https://www.healthline.com/health/mental-health/do-affirmations-work

Dogra, T. (2021, February 5). What is chakra meditation? Here's A guide to its physical and emotional benefits. OnlyMyHealth. https://www.onlymyhealth.com/chakra-meditation-guide-to-physical-emotional-health-benefits-1612504299

Dunn, S. T., Sinrich, J., Nelson, C., Clean Eating, & Smith, M. D. (2015, June 19). 10 reasons to eat clean. Clean Eating.

Erin Heger, S. C. (2020, December 16). 7 science-backed benefits of drinking water — and how much water you should drink each day. Insider. https://www.insider.com/benefits-of-drinking-water

Foods that absorb negative energy and the right way to use them. (2020, July 30). Times of India. https://timesofindia.indiatimes.com/life-style/food-news/foods-that-absorb-negative-energy-and-the-right-way-to-use-them/photostory/77244737.cms?picid=77245049

Girdwain, A. (2020, April 26). 5 benefits of sage, according to an herbalist. Well+Good. https://www.wellandgood.com/sage-benefits

Golden, J. (2020, January 29). 7 simple tools to clear negative energy from your space. Mindbodygreen. https://www.mindbodygreen.com/0-17791/7-simple-tools-to-clear-negative-energy-from-your-space.html

How cleanliness can affect your mental health. (2020, May 18). The Cleaning Collective. https://www.thecleaningcollective.co.uk/news/cleaning-tips/how-cleanliness-can-affect-your-mental-health

INTEGRIS Health. (n.d.). Make getting outside part of your daily routine. Integrisok.Com.

Moncel, B. (n.d.). Sage: An earthy flavor addition to a bounty of dishes. The Spruce Eats. https://www.thespruceeats.com/what-is-sage-1328645

Rekstis, E. (2022, January 21). Everything you need to know about healing crystals and their benefits. Healthline. https://www.healthline.com/health/mental-health/guide-to-healing-crystals

Saviuc, L. D. (2021, May 15). Shield and protect yourself from negative energies: Guided meditation. Purpose Fairy. https://www.purposefairy.com/76337/shield-yourself-negative-energies

Top 10 benefits of breathwork. (2020, February 24). Frequencymind.Com. https://www.frequencymind.com/blog/top-10-benefits-of-breathwork

View all posts by The Vibe With Ky. (2020, June 13). 3 benefits to speaking up for yourself. The Vibe With Ky. https://thevibewithky.com/2020/06/13/3-benefits-to-speaking-up-for-yourself

30 healing affirmations to help you achieve inner peace. (2018, May 29). ThinkUp App. https://thinkup.me/healing-affirmations

Nicholls, K. (2019, May 10). 6 tips to help protect your empath energy. Happiful Magazine. https://happiful.com/6-tips-to-help-protect-your-empath-energy

O'Connor, S., Indries, M., Varshney, P., Schettler, R. M., Hunter, F., & Husler, A. (2017, December 15). 16 yoga poses to keep you grounded & present. Yoga Journal.

Pizer, A. (n.d.). How Do You Do Tadasana, Yoga's Mountain Pose? Verywell Fit. https://www.verywellfit.com/mountain-pose-tadasana-3567127

The 54321 grounding technique for anxiety. (2020, June 29). Insight Timer Blog. https://insighttimer.com/blog/54321-grounding-technique

Borchard, T. J. (2010, March 28). 5 Gifts of Being Highly Sensitive. Psych Central. https://psychcentral.com/blog/5-gifts-of-being-highly-sensitive

lauraschwalm. (n.d.). The Spiritual Gifts of Empathy and Sensitivity (HSP). Pure Energy Healer https://pureenergyhealer.com/2013/10/17/the-spiritual-gift-of-empathy-and-sensitivity-hsp

Gaster, K. (2021, July 16). 6 Steps to Channeling Your Sensitivity as a Power. Highly Sensitive Refuge. https://highlysensitiverefuge.com/6-steps-to-channeling-your-sensitivity-as-a-power

The Differences Between Highly Sensitive People and Empaths. (n.d.). Psychology Today. https://www.psychologytoday.com/intl/blog/the-empaths-survival-guide/201706/the-differences-between-highly-sensitive-people-and-empaths

Granneman, J. (2014, October 18). 14 Advantages of Being Highly Sensitive. IntrovertDear.Com. https://introvertdear.com/news/highly-sensitive-person-advantages

Campbell, L. (n.d.). What Is an Empath and How Do You Know If You Are One? Verywell Mind https://www.verywellmind.com/what-is-an-empath-and-how-do-you-know-if-you-are-one-5119883

Scott, E. (n.d.). What Is a Highly Sensitive Person (HSP)? Verywell Mind. https://www.verywellmind.com/highly-sensitive-persons-traits-that-create-more-stress-4126393

STC. (2021, May 19). Living life as a highly sensitive person (HSP). Straight Talk Clinic. https://www.straighttalkcounseling.org/post/living-life-as-a-highly-sensitive-person-hsp